STRUGGLES OF FAITH

Struggles
of
Faith

Essays by
Michael Paul Gallagher SJ

THE COLUMBA PRESS
DUBLIN

First edition, 1990,
THE COLUMBA PRESS
93 The Rise, Mount Merrion, Blackrock, Co Dublin, Ireland.

Design by Bill Bolger
Origination by The Columba Press
Printed in Ireland by
Betaprint International Ltd., Dublin.

ISBN 0 948183 92 6

Acknowledgements:
The author and publisher gratefully acknowledge the co-operation of
the editors of the following journals, where essays were first published,
sometimes in different forms or under other titles:
Atheism Irish Style (*The Furrow,* 1974); What hope for Irish faith? (*The
Furrow,* 1978); Island of Slow Division (*Studies,* 1986); An Optimist-
Pessimist Dialogue (*America,* 1988); From Fate to Choice (*The Tablet,*
1989); An Anatomy of Religious Indifference (*The Month,* 1980); Secu-
larisation and New Forms of Faith (*Studies,* 1985);Walking with Unbe-
lievers (*The Way,* 1985); Imagination and Faith (*The Way,* 1984);Faith
Formation of Youth (*The Australasian Catholic Record,* 1987); The
Tone of Culture: From Prometheus to Narcissus (*Atheism & Dialogue,*
1989); Surprises of a Continent *and* Living Liberation (*The Tablet,*
1987); Assassination and St Anthony *and* Church of Clashing Symbols
(*The Tablet* 1989); Looking North at a World of Self (*America,* 1987);
What has Literature to say to Liturgy? (*Concilium,* 1980); Yeats, the
Mountain and the Temple (*The Month,* 1983); A Hopkins Centenary
Homily (*Studies,* 1989); Cheer for the Invisible (*The Tablet,* 1989); The
Gnostic Lure of Literature (*The Month, 1981*); Prayer: Ringing the
Changes (*The Furrow,* 1988)

Contents

*Modern people have lost sight of a freedom
enjoyed in every previous epoch,
that of being able to give themselves
to the time and the society in which they live.*
Andrey Tarkovsky

*The main challenge facing us has been
the absence of conventional supports
to make our life credible.
This, my friends, is the core of our solitude.*
Gabriel García Márquez

*Having confessed he feels
That he should go down on his knees and pray
For forgiveness for his pride, for having
Dared to view his soul from the outside.*
Patrick Kavanagh

*God has emerged again and again
in the history of wisdom
as the direction toward which wonder progresses.*
Michael J Buckley

Preface

The four quotations opposite are intended to set an agenda. They suggest that in the deeper things of life, ours has been a strangely deprived age. We have all the appearances of affluence – at least in the so-called developed world. But we have lost many of our anchors, many of our old tools of meaning. Worst of all, perhaps, we have been trained to trust only truth worked at 'from the outside', and hence to distrust the wisdom that is born from 'wonder'. That position of 'solitude' and detachment is our 'pride'and our poverty. It is a major cause of the troubles for faith that have been typical of our time.

Some people would wish to wave a magic wand and make all these pressures of modernity disappear. But there can be no such turning back of the clock. Instead we need to identify our troubles and search out honest ways to live our vision. The essays gathered here have that double project in view – to clarify the fate of faith and to seek authentic languages of Christianity for now.

Faith is the ability to survive one's moods – or so G.K.Chesterton remarked. His words easily apply to the struggles of individuals, as they run into periods when the whole 'God thing' seems utterly unreal. But his saying can equally fit the larger conflicts that faith has run into in modern times. A culture too has its versions of fatigue, or boredom, or disinterest. Quite often modern culture has been moody about religious faith, and one of the questions recurring in this book is how faith can find the capacity to survive those negative moods. Should it go underground, or back to the catacombs? After its flirtation with dialogue, should it now batten down the hatches of dogmatic securities, and expect the storms of confusion to pass eventually?

The answers found in these pages tend strongly towards keeping that dialogue with modernity open – and genuinely 'dialogue', in the sense of a two-way listening, and a two-way effort at understanding. An assumption throughout these pages is that it is good for faith to have to struggle, and that is true for individuals, countries, cultures, churches. No struggle, no life. Struggle may spell trouble at times, but without it there will be no aliveness.

The essays gathered here were written over the last fifteen years, but most of them belong to the decade of the eighties just ended. They were intended for different audiences – some more general and some more specialised. (The more notes, the more high-brow the implied reader!) Some were lengthy enough and some were short contributions for particular occasions. All of them have now been pruned for publication in book form. As the reader will immediately see, they are gathered here into sections, and each section has its own brief introduction. For anyone interested in the origin or date of any piece, the acknowledgements on page 2 provide that information. Two short pieces, a tribute to Samuel Beckett and the epilogue, have not been published before.

The general hope behind these pages is that if we can understand our situation more clearly, we can live with it more freely, and more creatively.

Rutilio Grande Community,
Ballymun.
January 1990

PART I: Are we losing the faith?

People will move away. They will of course go back to the Church for cultural occasions, but it may not be much more than that.

Raphael Gallagher, 1988

How drastic is this drift from traditional church belonging? The five articles included here span a period of fifteen years of reflecting on the faith situation in Ireland. 'Atheism Irish Style', the earliest one, dates from 1974 and is reprinted because at the time it caused a certain stir and has frequently been referred to since. In general these pieces reject any complacency about an easy continuity of faith in Ireland nowadays. Yet they remain basically optimistic as they seek out an honest language for the future.

Atheism Irish Style

It was Dr Johnson who remarked that the approach of death is wonderfully effective in forcing one to concentrate on the essentials of life. In this spirit I propose a meditation on the possible slow death of Irish Catholicism. The process may have begun in that significant numbers of young people are losing any living contact with both Christ and the Church. But the real crisis stems from ignoring this fact, from assuming that we can have the same continuity of Catholic practice as in the past.

In such a moment of confusion and change, older people are hurt because the young abandon what has been something sacred and central for them. Younger people often suffer too from their gradual entry into a horizon where the faith of their upbringing is no longer compatible with their experience; one of their most frequent questions is whether it is honest to continue to practise externally, simply to avoid upsetting their parents. A striking illustration of this may be found in John Broderick's novel *An Apology for Roses,* which explores the attitudes of the emerging middle class in a midlands town. In the closing pages of the novel, the young couple are planning their wedding. Religion seems irrelevant to them but they have to go through with the formula of a church marriage to please the family. Are they going to have to receive communion? That would mean confession, which would make each of them feel 'an awful hypocrite'. They decide to say nothing in advance but simply not to go to communion. And this particular conversation ends ironically with Marie warning Brian that he will have to conform and start going to Mass again after marriage:

'It isn't so bad once you get into the habit, which is all it is really. I don't think there's any point in making an issue of it. After all neither of us cares that much anymore. I wonder if anybody really does. And you meet people, keep up with the news and that sort of thing. Although of course the sermons are diabolical.'

This fictional situation can easily be mirrored in actuality. There seem to be many young couples hanging on to church practice for various reasons but with decreasing depth and commitment. No doubt many of them have higher motives than Marie and Brian. But it is far from unusual to hear them complain about the sheer drudgery of what is offered on Sunday in liturgy or preaching, and they often wonder how much longer they can continue. Needless to say their frustration and increasing apathy rubs off on their children.

Even already we have touched on what seems to be fairly central to 'atheism Irish style' – a disenchantment with the externals of church life and practice. Perhaps this is something peculiar to Irish unbelief at the moment, something which sets it off from international atheism. Certainly there are some Irish humanists and others who have thought out their position philosophically, but most young people who either reject religion or are drifting away from it are doing so on less sophisticated grounds. What one can call 'atheism Irish style' usually takes the form of alienation from the Church. By alienation I mean feelings of withdrawal, even of revulsion from something in which one is externally involved. Obviously alienation from externals can lead to the death of internals, in so far as those internals of faith in Christ were truly alive or mature in the first place.

Even if Church alienation is the primary and most frequent form of loss of faith in Ireland at the moment (and we can inquire into the causes in the next section), there are other kinds that should be mentioned. Apart from the intellectual unbeliever, touched on above, who moves away from faith through ideas, there is the psychological unbeliever, someone who finds faith impossible because of an unhappy life situation, someone who perhaps has never experienced love or self-acceptance and for whom the good news of Christ is too good to be true. Again, there are the political unbelievers who find the image of God as presented to them to be so other-worldly as to be irrelevant to the changes needed in society; God is rejected as an escapist fantasy, an underminer of urgency and human commitment. Of course there is the careless unbeliever who has drifted somewhat lazily and unthinkingly into his or her abandonment of faith or practice; until recently this person might be helped and supported by the presence of 'sociological Christianity', but if the tide now seems to be turning, the drift may well be in the opposite direction. One might speak also of the moral unbeliever, whose image of God is so exclusively that of a moral authority figure and who finds his commands so impossible to obey that it is better to ignore him. Another comparatively recent phenomenon may be called the religious unbeliever, someone who leaves the Church to pursue new cults, often of Eastern origin, or who joins fundamentalist Christian groups; the key factor here lies in an appeal to spiritual aspiration beside which the church practice of one's upbringing seems dead and superficial. Once again one comes back to an alienation from a seemingly externalist religion as a trait linking several forms of unbelief.

It is as well to acknowledge openly at this stage that the impressions outlined here are grounded in my own pastoral experience in the last few years. This has been largely but by no means exclusively concerned with university students. What I say in this article stems from hundreds of hours of conversation with boys and girls in their late teens and in their twenties. What I have found is that the bottom has fallen out of conventional faith for many of this age group. What their parents believe and practise sincerely as religion has turned them off. What they are taught as religion in school has gradually bored and even embittered them. What they experience for the most part in church on Sunday is a dull ritual that does not express anything meaningful for them. The result is that their image of Church and faith is not something worth growing into. So they 'lose faith', or perhaps more accurately they lose hope that what is presented as 'the faith' could ever again come alive in their lives. Many continue to practise with these doubts and reservations and sense of uninvolvement. Others quietly decide not to practise. Others again become quite explicit in their rejection of all that religion stands for.

If what I say is found pessimistic, I would gladly admit that I am presenting one side of the picture. There are many young people in Ireland today who are discovering a living faith and a deepened commitment to Christ in the Church and through the sacraments, or through less familiar channels such as prayer groups, youth organisations, christian encounter weekends, and the charismatic renewal movement. But my focus here is deliberately on the less hopeful aspects and if my message is deemed to be alarmist, I would prefer to be alarmist than complacent. The human realities as I view them are too serious for understatement. It seems to me inevitable that, within the coming decades, there is going to be a significant fall-off in religious faith among the younger age groups. What is already beginning to be visible in our statistics might have been dismissed as transitory, a passing aberration, a few years ago; now it is a human reality that has come to stay. So for the future I am pessimistic about quantity but optimistic about quality – because it seems clear that those who continue to believe and practice will need a greater degree of explicit Christian commitment than in previous generations. This is not to disparage in any sense the older ways of faith but simply to say that they are unlikely to prove viable in different conditions. To survive as a believer in the Ireland of the future a younger person will need to make a more conscious option for faith in the face of new opposing currents of unbelief.

Some Causes for the New Situation

If one tries to probe behind these new realities it is useful to distinguish at the outset between influences which are inevitable and factors that may lie within our responsibility as Christians. There is no point in blaming oneself for what could not have been prevented. Parents in particular are liable to suffer a lot of personal anguish in this respect, wondering if they are at fault when their children cast aside a practice of religion. So it needs to be said that a major cause lies in the culture in which we live. Ireland is no longer protected from the full brunt of the modern world, so that there is not a great deal of difference now between growing up in Dublin or in Birmingham so far as faith is concerned. Much relevant influence comes from the so-called 'youth culture', as embodied in music, life-style, clothes, changing attitudes on many fronts. 'What we're into is letting people know that they can get it together', to quote a hippy-type expression of a new mood. The new outlook, getting it together, places great value on liberating experiences that can be both deeply inward and shared with others. Many of the ways of doing this may be unacceptable or shallow or self-deceptive. But one positive point seems clear: this youth culture is far from materialistic in any naïve sense. Its values may be anti-conventional but they are far from anti-religious. The problem arises because the new stress on personal liberation and intensified experience does not seem answered by conventional religion.

What, then, are some of the specifics in Irish Catholicism that allow this alienation to take hold? They may be summarised under three headings: trouble in the teaching of religion in schools; failings in the pastoral ministry of the Church; and weakness in the quality of Christian living in families and in Irish society.

One does not have to go deep in conversation with someone who has dropped religion to find often a resentment against both school and Church. Both are accused of what may be called the externalist heresy – putting so much emphasis on external conformism as to contradict their proper Christian purpose. Many young people, even in recent years, seem to have been taught their faith in school in an authoritarian and aggressive way. More seriously still they have been taught it in a highly impersonal way, as if it were like mathematics, or the vocabulary of some foreign language, or something to be learned off by heart. The teaching seems to have been geared more to correctness of doctrine and conformism of practice than to conversion of life and heart. Of course Christian doctrine has to be taught and the content of the faith clarified; but all this activity is doomed to irrelevance if it assumes a faith that may no longer be there even in secondary school. Religious teaching is bound to fail if there is no attempt to offer an experience of faith, of prayer, of living worship as the personal and communal basis for it all. No doubt new modes of catechetics are helpful nowadays and no doubt many teachers of religion of all ages have done marvellous work in communicating not only doctrine but their own enthusiastic commitment to Christ and Church. There still remain too many religious classrooms that are disaster areas for faith.

That the human failures of the Church can be a cause of atheism was acknowledged, at least in an indirect way, by the Vatican Council. Atheism 'is not a spontaneous development but stems from a variety of causes, including a critical reaction against the christian religion'. And in this process 'believers can have more than a little to do with the birth of atheism' (*Gaudium et Spes*, 19). In similar vein, Yves Congar looks on modern atheism less as a shutting out of God than as a rejection of how he has been presented. In much unbelief today, Father Congar says, it is what we have done with religion rather than God that is being rejected. Ireland too is beginning to show signs of that paradoxical international development of recent years: an upsurge of interest in religious experience as seen in Jesus movements and meditation schools, and at the same time a loss of credibility by institutional religion. Irish-style atheism, as already mentioned, is seldom professed atheism at all but an unbelief in the Church or an inability to see it as mediating anything alive or liberating.

Thus the question becomes, to what extent these negative images of the Church in the minds of young people are grounded in real failures by the Church? 'In the beginning was the word and the word was No': thus opens a short story by Brian Moore, looking back on his Catholic upbringing in Belfast, and wittily capturing a moralistic and repressive experience of religion. 'It is now immoral to say 'yes' to an institution which by its preoccupation with irrelevancies is diverting people from God': these are angry words from a secondary school student. 'The older you get the more you realise just how easy it is to live without the Church's brand of religion': this comes from an ex-seminarian. 'What the Church seems to ask of me is so much on the surface that it does nothing for me. I do it when I'm at home for the sake of my mother, but I feel infantile and dishonest': a girl, now a teacher, from a small town background.

Externalism on its own is a real danger. But there is a third, less tangible area concerning the fruits of religion in daily life and in society. Many of the younger generation say that they are fed up hearing about religion, but they are not fed up seeing it lived. What they find is a religion often divorced from social realities, a pietism that literally makes no earthly difference. And this does not answer their aspirations. In all this perhaps much of the weakness of Irish Catholicism for young people stems from an extraordinary amount of emphasis being put on attendance at Mass and at the same time an impoverished practice of the Eucharist. It can often be reduced to an individualistic duty with little or no relevance. It can be performed as a mere ritual with little attempt to create a human community among those present. It can assume a prayerfulness and a faith that may no longer exist. It can fail to bring about any genuine transformation of life or to awaken any social conscience in the community. These, at least, are some possible causes underlying our present difficulties.

How to Respond?

The essential response, and not always an easy one, is to face the facts. If this were done, we might have no difficulty over pastoral changes because we would find Ireland to be a missionary country in a new sense. It would be no longer possible to assume that a congregation has 'the faith' firmly alive or that an unbeliever in a secondary school is merely an oddity. Recognition of the growing crisis would almost automatically change our wavelength of thinking and communicating and planning for the future. But the ostrich posture is tempting – to evade the writing on the wall, keeping the head down in safe unshifting sand.

This final section will be brief and can offer only general guidelines. First of all, it may help to distinguish three possible reactions among those who want to admit the overall picture as outlined here. For want of better labels they may be called the conservative, liberal, and the radical models. The conservative response is to argue and to judge, to say 'you should go to Mass and here are the reasons', to treat individuals to a kindly dose of advice. This well-intentioned approach may easily fail in terms of 'wavelength', by not paying enough attention to the new world in which youth lives. This often applies to parents who feel a duty to argue with their children over religious practice. If growth is the aim, argument is out of place. Even good theological reasons may prove beside the point. If young people are complaining about religion on the level of human experience, an answer on the level of understanding does not meet them. The conservative wavelength often fails because it does not listen enough to appreciate the quite different starting point for questions of faith among the younger generation.

The liberal approach, on the other hand, is clear that one does not want to be repressive, to impose beliefs on anyone, that one wants to understand people and to listen, to be open to new questions; but the danger is that one may never get beyond listening to speaking, that one is so liberal as to forget the urgency of the gospel. Once again the wavelength of communication has been inadequate, in that it has not been honestly mutual.

What I would advocate as the radical response would avoid mere advice and judging, and mere acceptance. It would ground itself in two New Testament realities, witness and conversion. It would try to share a personal witness of word and life, with the hope of preparing the way for conversion of others to living faith in Christ.

My key terms, then, are witness, wavelength, and conversion. By witness I mean not just good example but something more demandingly personal and visible. It would cover the witness, not only of an individual, but of a community, a Church. The teacher and preacher have now to be seen to live what they teach and to be personally caught up in what they preach. The first apostles were personal witnesses to Christ, they were not teachers of religion out of books. And there is a vital link between witness and wavelength. If the witness is real, the problem of wavelength will often take care of itself. By stressing wavelength, I mean that the context of communication today needs as much attention as the content. This would apply to teaching, sermons, and family discussions of religion. An excellent article by Denis Rice, himself a parent, talks about teenagers in these terms: 'I should speak to them primarily through our experience of the home and family. The only authority that will take them to God is the authority of their own experience; and particularly, their experience of people who claim to know and love him.' Drawing on the same article, one might suggest that the main pastoral programme we need is not so much a dramatic apostolate for the young themselves, but, through the schools, a real campaign of adult education for their parents, helping them 'to explore where they are in their own belief', as Mr Rice puts it (*Clergy Review*, October 1973).

Finding the appropriate wavelength and having the courage to offer personal Christian witness, are both aimed at helping mature conversion to Christ. Too much emphasis has been put in the past on religion as involving obedience to specific activities and practices. In a new culture that kind of practice cannot continue without internal conviction. So the pastoral focus has to change from being content with continuity of practice to preparing for more explicit commitment of faith. Up to now much teaching and preaching seemed to assume that continuity of practice was possible and sufficient. It was never sufficient and in our new situation it may not be possible either, unless rooted in some adult conversion. In many cases the young people who are rejecting Church practice may not be rejecting Christ at all, for the simple reason that they may never have experienced him as real or as the living Lord.

What I have said needs balancing in many ways – but I am convinced that it needs saying even as it stands. It needs balancing by the fact that the depth of faith in many young people is truly growing. They are moving into that personal degree of commitment in and through the Church, that alone can survive the new climate of secularism. It is mediocrity that cannot survive. It is mere externalism that will die. But that is not the real Church or the real faith. Many, of course, as the phrase goes, are throwing out the baby with the bathwater. They lose personal faith because they lose confidence in the institution, and this is a cause of sadness and self-questioning. But the process of loss may ultimately be purifying, if we come to see that the faith needs less our defence of it than our living of it.

What I have been calling atheism Irish style may be a purgative stage on the way to some new faith Irish style. If it is to be just a purgative stage, the present situation has to be faced and urgently. Time is not on our side. But Ireland still has an enormous potential for not losing the faith.

What Hope for Irish Faith?

When the main body of this paper was given as a lecture at the Conference of Irish Priests, one of the groups asked, 'Why do you think religion in Ireland will not go the same way as other western countries?' Having been given the assignment of presenting a sober account of the problem areas for faith today, it was a pleasant surprise to be called on to defend one's optimism. My answer was conditional. If little is done by way of renewal, then Ireland could easily become yet another example of minority religion; but this need not happen. Especially if a new pastoral creativity can be encouraged among priests, Ireland still has an excellent chance of retaining a people's Church.

The argument will be that hope for Irish faith in the future depends on (a) seeing the new dangers as clearly as possible; (b) admitting the inadequacy of older responses; and (c) building anew on the uniquely strong situation that still exists.

New Society Induces Shallow Faith

In April 1974, I wrote a piece called 'Atheism Irish Style'. Looking back now it still seems true but its model of belief and unbelief was very personalist: it stemmed mainly from pastoral work with individuals. It may be relevant to mention that my own most important experience in the intervening years was five months in India, working with Mother Teresa and also learning something of eastern approaches to prayer. On my return I was forced to see the Irish faith situation in much more social terms than before. I also began to sense a possible spiritual malnutrition behind the impressive Church practice in Ireland: malnutrition is not starvation but rather a hunger that remains unrecognised, a hunger cloaked by finding food but food of a poor kind, ultimately lacking in nourishment. The two levels – social and spiritual – seemed to converge into an awareness that in Ireland now the immediate danger to faith is not unbelief but shallow belief. Coming back to Ireland from the poor world highlighted for me the sheer materialism of our environment and the fact that since the boom of the sixties affluence has created a completely different context of values and life-styles, different even from the fifties. Economics has quietly but inevitably replaced religion as the dominant value in Irish society. This social change has created a new context not openly at war with Christianity but in fact hostile to the survival of real faith. Our social context for the future is one where increasingly greed and envy will be valued and cultivated in glossy forms. In this world the danger is that religion be reduced to a minor leisure-time activity, a convention retained but only on the margins of life, something devoid of challenge or depth.

But there are two sides to this quiet faith crisis in Ireland: a whole cluster of social changes has created a more problematic outer context for religion, but there is also the inner or Church context. The Sunday fidelity in Ireland is the outstanding fact here, something extraordinary by international standards and which must be a real source of hope. It is the key strength from which to build for a more complex future. But, to adapt Marx, a full church could be the opium of the clergy: it could blind one not only to the growing absenteeism but to the hidden spiritual malnutrition of those present. Precisely because of the drastically changed outer context, Sunday practice need no longer lead to strong faith. In a more secular Ireland, unsupported Sunday practice may easily fail to nourish a mature religious life. It will require many new forms of support activities if faith is to avoid shallowness and ultimately unbelief.

Sower Parable and Ireland Now
One could re-read the parable of the sower in the light of these new dangers in the outer and inner contexts of Irish religion. We have our versions of the birds of the air, the hostile forces that cause a diminishing and even a collapse of faith. One is familiar with the distinction between secularisation and secularism: the first has to do with the increasing separation of roles and controls between Church and civil society; the second usually means a denial of anything beyond the secular or this-worldly horizon. Thus where the first can be natural and, at least in theory, positively purifying for faith, the second involves a rejection of faith and of God.

To what extent will the inevitable secularisation of Ireland lead to secularism? Cardinal Danielou once warned that 'in a completely secularised society, it would be impossible for Christianity to be accessible to the poor'– in the sense of people who may not have the tools or opportunities for making personal religious choices. There are ambiguous forces at work in Irish society in recent years that are, to say the least, insensitive to religious values. The birds of the air come in various disguises.

We also have our versions of the shallow earth of the parable, the earth where roots are weak and withering predictable. In many ways this would fit the inner context of Church life: it is hard to realise that where sowing the seed two inches down brought forth fruit in the past, two inches may be dangerously little in modern storm conditions. In so far as Irish Catholicism remains on the level of individualist piety rather than social concern, or on the level of convention rather than conviction, it is unlikely to survive as a strong majority Church in a more secular environment.

Thirdly, it is only too easy to identify our current forms of the choking thorns. Christ himself names them as a desire for riches with all its attendant distractions from God. Within a mere fifteen years , Ireland has been swamped by a new consumerism, and as in the case of secularisation, it is a question of something potentially good being also potentially dangerous. The expansion of the economy is one thing but being bombarded by the subtle propaganda of big business is another. It thrives on trivialisation, sells superficiality and deadens the deeper springs of religious awareness.

Thus one can, fairly crudely, name the three elements of the parable as they apply today: the birds become secularisation veering in some confusion towards secularism; shallow earth can be caused by failure of pastoral imagination within the Church itself; the thorns today show themselves in the life-patterns of a consumer society, a relatively new phenomenon in Ireland.

Throughout the western world in recent years, youth has become almost a new social class with its own norms and peer language. 'You were never my age' is a quite justifiable retort by a twenty-three year old of today to a parent or teacher or priest in their forties, who tries to begin a sentence of advice with:'When I was your age...' This unprecedented differentness of culture and environment inevitably relativises the more traditional forms of religious practice. In fact Yves Congar, the distinguished French theologian, has spoken of this youth culture as the most important 'new reality' unforeseen by the Vatican Council and yet of crucial importance in its impact on the future of the faith. The question is whether the twentieth-century Church will lose the young, just as the nineteenth-century Church lost the working class in most countries of Europe. An accountancy student recently pinpointed the change for me by saying that among his peers he is more likely to be asked with surprise why he goes to Mass than why he does not. In many young circles in Ireland today, non-practice is increasingly the peer norm; and in the context of the powerful influence of the whole youth culture, this peer pressure can be as decisive as family, church and school put together.

A second social force is urbanisation and it has been a world-wide experience that the decline in rural populations has been accompanied by a decline in religious adherence. The city is the place that corresponds to the shallow earth of the sower parable, a place of weak roots, where people are exposed to the typical modern experiences of being adrift in an anonymous place and of being unsupported in their human and religious aspirations. The old sustaining social context of the rural parish is no longer viable in the town. The urban relativism of life-style undermines the old securities. As E. F. Schumacher argued in his classic, *Small is Beautiful,* the upper limit for humane community is a city of half a million inhabitants; the changing situation in Dublin in recent years would seem to verify his thesis.

As in the example of youth culture, so too in the case of urbanisation, what the Church is experiencing is less a crisis of faith than a crisis of culture. The surrounding culture of a new generation has meant that they are often inevitably 'turned off' by organised religion as it has been experienced by them. They are equally and painfully adrift from other inherited values; the assumptions of parents and teachers in many areas of life are also under question. In Ireland in particular the drift from religious practice does not necessarily mean the arrival of atheism. Just as it is more accurate to speak of a communication gap than of a generation gap, so it is more important to recognise a crisis in the languages and forms of religion rather than a crisis of the contents of faith.

On the strength of Irish Catholic practice there is no need to cite statistics. The eloquent fact is that in no subgroup, so far dealt with in surveys, is there any clear majority of people entirely lapsed from faith or practice. This constitutes a majority report that can give immense hope for the future. It confirms that, even among younger generations, substantial majorities show signs of fidelity to the Church and of openness to religious growth. Of course there are minorities, even substantial ones, who seem to be opting out of Catholicism and some are unlikely to return. The future will certainly see some families of Irish ex-Catholics bringing up their children without baptism and outside Church contact – it is happening already. The future will also hear more atheist voices raised in protest against the majority consensus. (On this point Irish Catholicism could be in danger of developing a right-wing backlash response towards such deviants, even within a family situation: this would be quite out of harmony with the universal Church's commitment to understanding and dialogue with unbelievers today.) As Fr Liam Ryan has written recently, Ireland in the 1980's may perhaps see a higher presence of both marginal believers and liberal Catholics, those unhappy with Church authority but the 'orthodox', he predicts, 'will continue to be in the majority'. Thus a double pastoral question will face Irish priests: how can one develop the potentials for Christian maturity in the majority, and, simultaneously how can one understand and meet the needs of minorities who are drifting from faith and practice?

Of course the key question for the future of the faith is not minimum external convention but some level of conviction and maturity. The older patterns of quasi-universal religious practice, still found in rural areas, can involve a certain degree of social conformism. When that conformism loses its power, as it has done for younger and urbanised families, a quite different pastoral approach is called for. Irish Catholics seem to be over-sacramentalised and under-evangelised. Sacramental attendance is experienced by many as a matter of obedience or duty rather than as a spiritual nourishment or meeting with the Lord. Similarly among university students I have found an amazing ignorance of scripture: many do not possess a copy of the New Testament. To trust in a simple continuity of older pastoral methods would be to court irrelevance in the eyes of the drifting minorities; but it could also court a disastrous shallowness in the case of the orthodox majority. What is needed is a courageous application of many of the renewal methods that have been developed abroad for more difficult situations. To cite Bishop Cahal B Daly: 'These movements of renewal can be more effective in a society of high religious practice, such as Ireland, than in one which has been already massively secularised. I believe that conciliar renewal can be more efficacious as a preventive of de-Christianisation than as a remedy for it.'

Triple Renewal and Triple Decline

Putting it very simply there seem to be three main thrusts of renewal in the worldwide Church today, and these three could have a special application in the unique situation of Ireland: spiritual renewal, small support groups, and social commitment. As against these new potentials, one can discern three new dangers, three forms of lapsing from religion: apathy, alienation and anger.

To expand on that rather schematic thesis, let us start with the three dangers. Apathy is a form of socio-cultural loss of faith. It is largely passive: it stems from a new environment dominated by money-values and this in turn results in a dull indifference to the spiritual dimension of life. The American poet, Howard Nemerov, has questioned 'whether it is possible for a religious attitude to exist in the acceptance of prosperity, and with its face set against suffering'. Apathy to religion can co-exist with religious practice even within the one family or person or parish. It means that behind the church-going the religious question can be largely dead, real prayer non-existent and there is a pervasive sense of unreality about God. Apathy is a kind of drifting with the social tide, with the secular environment that is uninterested rather than hostile towards faith. To sit for hours each evening before the superficialities of television is a sure recipe for apathy, not just on the religious front. To allow oneself to be kidnapped by the consumerist way of life, the bourgeois paradise, leads ultimately to an untroubled, unconscious, even casual inner abandoning of the Christian faith. As St Paul put it to Timothy: they will keep the outer forms of religion but will reject its inner power (2 Tim 3:5). The pastoral answer to apathy lies in various forms of spiritual renewal, which can restore faith from the margins of life to its centre. Statistics show that even among young people a good proportion have some form of daily prayer. But a layman who took part in one of the discussions at the Galway Conference of Priests surprised his group by saying he had never heard a sermon on prayer, not even a bad one. There seems to be a spiritual hunger that is not being answered through any adequate initiation into prayer either in school or church; the immense spiritual experimentation among religious in recent years, with courses, directed retreats, prayer workshops and so on, does not seem to have borne fruit as yet in their apostolates. So there remains a huge potential for growth in spiritual education for our more secular Ireland. A reawakening and deepening of prayer life is a sure antidote to apathy, since a person who learns genuine prayer will not only be less deceived by the consumerist drift of his surroundings, he or she will discover a hidden treasure, a way of belonging within the reality of being loved by God – which is the opposite of trivialisation and apathy.

Distance through Disenchantment

Alienation by comparison with apathy is more agitated or troubled in mind and conscience. It is less a form of drifting than a definite disappointment with institutional life within the Church. It often arises from precise sources of dissatisfaction with conventional religion and with the priests and religious who are viewed as embodiments of this convention. For the 'alienated', the religious question is far from dead, but forms of worship and of preaching are found to be 'boring', 'irrelevant', 'annoying', 'more a nuisance than a help'. A national report on 'Youth, culture and the Faith' drawn up in 1974 spoke of 'disillusionment' with the Church rather than unbelief as a serious problem. Such necessary activities as fund-raising were singled out for criticism: a priest's 'well-meaning and unselfish devotion to raising up a worthy edifice for the worship of the Lord may well be the very factor responsible for emptying it'. At the Galway Conference the paper given by Fr Brian D'Arcy expanded at some length, and with courageous vehemence, on the 'image of a sterile institution' experienced by many young people.

Such alienation can perhaps best be met by many forms of small group renewal within the large Church. As Schumacher put it, 'the fundamental task is to achieve smallness within a large organisation'. Translating this into the situation of Irish Catholicism means that there is an urgent need for church cells larger than the family but smaller than the parish. Once again it means transposing to our healthy climate one of the key pastoral insights of the international church today: the Synod on catechetics gave special encouragement to

21

'basic communities', ways of finding support for one's faith with small groups of others in mutual commitment. The Galway Conference heard much mention of marriage encounter, scripture groups, new-style parish retreats in this regard, and the paper presented by Fr Séamus Ryan made an eloquent plea for supplementing traditional parish activities with forms of exposing people to the real life of the Church, through 'prayer and witness and service'.

From Pietism to Commitment

The third umbrella term to describe loss of faith is 'anger'. This is at the opposite end of the spectrum from apathy in that it is much more active, conscious, chosen and ideological in its stance. Apathy is a danger for a large number of people. Alienation affects mainly the more searching and the more educated, an increasing proportion in Irish society. Anger applies as yet only to a small but important fringe. It would subdivide into at least two major forms of vocal and even vehement rejection, not only of the Church, but of Christian faith itself. On the one hand there are the various kinds of intellectual rejection of faith. On the other hand there is the more socio-political anger with a religion of mere piety or mere obligation. As mentioned earlier there is a particular Irish danger of not hearing the truth behind this anger and of dismissing it as unfounded and irresponsible. Pope Paul VI, in his encyclical *Ecclesiam Suam*, spoke of such atheists today as 'sometimes men of great breadth of mind, impatient with mediocrity and self-seeking'. In Ireland a lot of anger is caused by the credibility gap between the content of the Gospel and the life-styles of priests and religious. The Church is accused of preaching justice in words alone but of doing little to confront or change social ills.

Once again the pastoral response here can be an Irish adaptation of some of the exciting developments in the universal Church, in particular some application of the theologies of liberation in both the thinking and actions of Irish Catholics. As well as the spiritual and the small group, the social dimension will need new expression for a time of northern violence, affluence and unemployment. The Church will need not only to offer verbal critiques of injustice but to work for alternative ways of family life and of involvement in social change and in Christian peace-making. Religious congregations in particular can give a lead in actually sharing the life of the deprived and then, with the authority of lived experience, they can awaken more effectively the conscience of the rest of the Church.

Discerning the future

I tried to suggest earlier a re-reading of the parable of the sower. One could summarise some of the conclusions by a similar treatment of the twin parables of building the tower and preparing for battle

(Lk 14). Their burden concerns discernment, planning, and a realistic sense of one's hopes and dangers. The tower could be left incomplete and jagged if one does not realise the newness of the situation within which faith has now to be built. It needs new bricks and new methods of construction. In many respects the cultural tide has turned and will no longer offer the same support for religious faith. There will be less reliance on authority and custom and much more on interiorisation and commitment. Again, there can be two hypotheses about the battle of the future. According to one version, the enemy only appears strong to a few prophets of doom and so the future of Irish Catholicism seems easily assured – even though it may fray a bit more at the edges. According to another report from the scouts sent forward to survey the field, the enemy is playing a waiting game and can pounce suddenly and without warning. Between 1971 and 1975 Mass-going in France fell by a massive 40%, or 10% per annum. Surely a middle position is what is required. If the Irish church can read the strengths and dangers of the present faith situation, and can give courageous priority to the new pastoral needs, then a certain guarded optimism about the future is well justified.

Innovation has always been a hallmark of Irish missionaries abroad: it is a question of the same missionary zeal and adventure being brought to bear on the local situation. The causes of lessening of practice and belief lie in two directions – both in the inevitabilities of the age and in the human failures of ourselves as witnesses of the Gospel. Just as EEC regulations slowly eroded our freedom on fisheries, so also many large forces in our western world erode our freedom as fishers of faith. But within our own hands is the question of the trawlers and nets we use within our own waters. As fishers of faith we may be less free than we were but more free than we know.

Island of Slow Division

In mid-June 1986 BBC Radio 4 broadcast an eighty-minute programme called 'Ireland – Myth and Message'. Its opening words
were 'you can't get away from religion in Ireland'. The discussion
went on to illustrate the many ways in which this island is uniquely
unsecular and in which Catholicism in particular retains a significant
place in most people's lives. Exactly a week after the broadcast, its
picture seemed massively confirmed by the results of the divorce
referendum; at least the British perception of that event was that the
Church had defeated the progressives. On reflection a more nuanced
analysis is called for, not only of the referendum but of the religious
situation that Ireland finds herself in as the second millenium
approaches.

Most infants baptised this coming year will be in their teens after
the symbolic year of 2000. It is unlikely that they will find it so hard
to 'get away from religion'. In an eloquent contribution to the BBC
programme, Seamus Deane evoked his own upbringing in Derry in
the forties and fifties, where 'being a Catholic' was a 'saturating experience' and an 'affectionate womb'. No doubt that saturation was
true in other urban families up to the fifties. Perhaps it may still
describe some aspects of rural Ireland in the eighties. But it will surely
not be the environment for the teenagers of 2000, partly because it is
less and less a reality for their parents today.

Which brings me to the implications of my title. Everyone predicted
that the divorce referendum would show a division between Dublin
and the rest of the country. It did that, but much less so than expected,
and that is one indicator of what I mean by 'slow' division. In spite of
having had a period of rapid social change since the sixties, Ireland is
undergoing a remarkably slow secularisation, at least by international
standards. Externally at least the somewhat similar religiousness of
Spain seems to have declined much more dramatically in a shorter
span of time. The process of change in Ireland has resulted in widen-
ing gaps between groups of people and that is what this short essay
wants to explore. The main divisions are fairly obvious: urban–rural;
south–north; young–old; unemployed–employed; comfortable–
deprived. Our question here is how this slow division alters the
previously saturated culture behind Irish religion.

Two Cultures

I remember talking to a Polish priest some years ago, at the time
of the resurgence of national feeling there through *Solidarity*. I asked
him how it was that religion seemed so universally popular in Poland

whereas, in the 'free world', it is largely in decline as an influence in society. His answer was unhesitating and crystal clear: 'we in Poland have the advantage of a visible enemy in the shape of a totalitarian state, but you in the West have the disadvantage of an invisible enemy, one hard to identify so clearly – all the allurements of a superficial lifestyle'. The implication was that if only we could see our enemy, and know his power, we too would form a new *Solidarity*. We would want to join the resistance.

One rather optimistic reading of the referendum result was that it presented a courageous decision to be different. If so, it would need to be accompanied by many another option to join the resistance to the Americanising way of life and to create a genuinely caring society. There is not much evidence that Ireland has the will to refuse to be swamped by the familiar idols of capitalist culture – competitive success, pleasure dominance, protection of the already privileged, and privatised religiousness. By the yardstick of a divorce referendum or by the yardstick of Church attendance, Ireland seems a powerfully Church-reverencing society. My question here is whether these measurements are not relatively uncostly and in the long term not very significant as indicators of the spiritual state of a nation. Behind the slow division and the slow secularisation a more radical cultural shift is taking place. It would be far too innocent to speak of faith without adverting to this context.

From a religious point of view, the most crucial division in Irish society was not covered in our list of two paragraphs back. It is the divide between two cultures in contemporary Ireland – between those for whom the world of Church remains nourishing and those for whom it has become empty and even incredible. It is not a theological crisis in any strict sense; indeed a certain theological illiteracy is characteristic of most people in both camps. What is at stake is the plausibility of the human language of religion: for different people it is either managing or failing to make sense within a changed world.

Strengths and Weaknesses

What then are some of the strengths and weaknesses of Church life in Ireland now? In answering this question it has to be admitted in advance that our focus will (unfortunately) be limited to a mainly southern and Catholic perspective. The strengths can be outlined as follows:[1]

- a Church that retains popular loyalty to a degree unknown elsewhere in Europe;
- a tradition of Sunday worship that remains strong even in the younger generation (some three quarters of Catholics in their twenties attend Mass weekly):

- nearly 30 per cent of people in the Republic go to Mass more frequently than weekly, and for reasons of personal conviction;
- a major impact by religion on the educational system, at least up to the end of second level;
- a population that prays frequently (over 80 per cent have some daily prayer);
- even if vocations have declined, the resource of large numbers of priests and religious, many of them highly trained;
- the development in recent years of successful courses in theology for lay people in many parts of the country;
-an inherited sense of Christian belonging in most families, and hence homes that communicate faith;
- an openness to renewal and variety of experiment in areas of youth ministry;
- a new sensitivity to justice issues, at least in official positions and in some religious groups;
- a new awareness of the Christian vision of liberation in the Third World and a justifiable pride in the participation of Irish men and women in the struggle.

No doubt many other positive areas could be mentioned; these are given merely as a selection. What of the weakness or dangers?
- the poor motivation of the majority for their regular church-going, i.e. legalistic reasons for obeying a 'duty'or avoiding a sin;
- pastoral failure of Sunday Mass attendance to nourish mature faith;
- 'unlike most countries, levels of belief are lower than levels of religious practice', thus suggesting a certain social conformism (*Máire Nic Ghiolla Phádraig*),[2]
- the lack of a sense of community in most parishes, particularly in urban areas;
- the combination of an over-clericalised Church and a passive laity creating a situation of pastoral immobility;
- the alienation of significant sub-groups, particularly the urban-educated and the young-unemployed;
- the shortage of young clergy and religious and, in many senior personnel, a lack of confidence in dealing with the large new generation;
- 'the image of religion as obscurantist and of the Church as an institution protecting its own power'(*Bishop Donal Murray*);[3]
- the failure of most second-level religious education to foster an alert understanding of faith;
- confusion of parents, caught between different models of religion, who lack confidence in their own faith and hence give double messages in their families;

- the lingering impression of a puritan religion that remains negative towards sexuality and authoritarian in its norms in this area.
- the image of a devotional religion that has little impact on social realities and choices.

What emerges from these litanies is a picture once again of 'slow division'. All the Irish Churches retain a high degree of traditional respect and even affection. At least this is the case for the vast majority of Irish people and even for decent majorities among the younger generation. The roots remain firm – on the surface; and that deliberate paradox may express a significant truth. Irish Catholicism may be handicapped by its very bigness and prevented from being able to meet the new and varied needs of minorities within its orbit. The majority may remain satisfied with the average diet while that very diet is the source of disillusionment and anger for others. To continue much the same metaphor, the situation of outer health may conceal a quite dangerous malnutrition of various kinds. Intellectually, few of the younger generation seem able to 'give the account of the hope that is in them'(as Peter asked in the New Testament). Pastorally, sacraments without evangelised faith may prove empty or fruitless in the long term. Spiritually, the very success of devotionalism can miss the hunger for a deeper prayer life as experienced by many today. Communally, the full churches can mask both the fact of many absentees among the young and the lack of genuine contact between those present. Socially, in spite of many excellent documents and speeches, the Churches appear marginal and even impotent when faced with the twin evils of unemployment and violence. Culturally, most church activities seem geared toward preservation of the faithful rather than towards diversity of ministry and outreach to those becoming distanced in different ways from the faith-roots of their fathers and mothers.

Sociological and Psychological Perspectives
Professor Liam Ryan has put a lucid finger on the source of the slow division that we are exploring. Writing in *The Tablet* for a St Patrick's Day issue in 1985, he pointed out that in 'a single generation Ireland has moved away from a situation where all the influences fashioning the lives of people converged on a unified interpretation of life'.[4] The outcome, in his view, has been that 'values and beliefs are increasingly a matter of choice, less a matter of tradition' and in particular that 'religion has become a much less certain matter'. This would seem to link up with Alasdair McIntyre's insight that changes in the social community are the principal sources of changes in religious consciousness. When the old cohesiveness begins to fragment, what we are calling a situation of slow division takes over, and in such a situation some people move away faster and further than others. Precisely

because of this uneven mobility, the Churches find themselves faced with much less homogeneous congregations present at their worship and, among the non-practising, varying degrees of disenchantment with the whole Church 'scene' can be found. This multiplicity is new to the Church in Ireland; they have been accustomed to a more unified flock. Rather than find ways of coping with this challenging diversity of needs, the temptation is to continue to offer the traditional menu for the many who still want it, and quietly to ignore the increasing minorities who have different and more difficult religious needs.

Out of this new sociological environment for religion in Ireland comes the need for a different level of 'faith develoment', a term popularised by James Fowler, an American psychologist-theologian.[5] He holds that the language of faith naturally changes and expands through the phases of each individual lifespan: what begins as the basic trust of the infant later becomes the story-loving of the young child. While this is not the moment to go into his several 'stages of faith', one particular transition seems relevant to the Irish religious situation. What Fowler calls 'stage three' is normally the language of adolescent faith, which can then evolve into 'stage four' during early adulthood. Fowler argues that most religious institutions are more comfortable when their people stay within stage three and do not make the transition to the fuller maturity of stage four. Stage three is characterised by a mixture of emotional solidarity within a group and a certain inarticulate acceptance of authority from beyond the self. This fits with the unquestioning fidelity to a Church that has been an important strand in Irish identity for several generations now. The tone was one of loyal obedience rather than of critical choice. Beneath what was often dismissed from the outside as slavish passivity, this language of faith could nourish a deep sense of God as friend; because the outer structures were firm, they fostered an often hidden prayer relationship to God and a flourishing spirituality of sacraments.

Fowler's stage three type of faith was most naturally at home in Ryan's older and more unified society. But the new social situation evoked by Ryan would seem to require the faith development of Fowler's stage four. An older Ireland, with its stabilities, could arrive at depth and maturity of religious commitment through the more Church-reliant assumptions of stage three. But the new Ireland of slow division that has emerged since 1960 has produced many people who will need another wavelength of religion if their faith is to survive the trials of a more complex culture. If Churches keep people within the familiar dependence of stage three, that could now result

in immaturity and could alienate people by disappointing their hopes
for more suitable spiritual nourishment. Fowler's stage four is focused
on encouraging a faith of personal decision rather than of more conventional belonging. If the teenager lives in a world of relationships, of
groping identity, of conformity to the group, the young adult devel-
ops capacities for making responsible choices and living them out.
Thus the faith-language of stage four is one of more explicit or conscious commitment, one that is less dependent on support structures
and more able to swim against the tide. This stage of development
calls for people to stand more confidently on their own feet and hence
to cope with a new diversity of attitudes and lifestyles around them.

Six Challenges

The liberation theologian, Juan Luis Segundo, speaks of the transition from a closed society to an open society as bringing about a crucial challenge to the language of faith. He insists on the new 'urgent
task of winning personal conviction'.[6] But he goes further in discerning some of the dangers of any in-between situation. He points to a
subtle temptation to 'maintain consumer majorities who are artificially
bound to Christianity'. This means that in order to keep the maxi-
mum number of people, religion becomes a tranquillising but unchallenging activity on the margins of life. In this scenario the open society
has no difficulty in retaining a vague and shallow version of Church
life and avoiding the cutting edge of the Gospel. 'What happens in the
case of people who receive some dogmatic corpus but no good
news?''Do people become free human beings?'These questions form
what might be called a liberation litmus test for our Irish situation
also.

In the light of all that has been said, it is possible to summarise the
Irish religious situation as facing six major challenges during the closing years of this century.

First, there is the challenge of diversity which has been stressed here:
how are the Churches to learn to live respectfully and fruitfully with
those who have different needs from the mainstream of the faithful?

Secondly, and connected with this diversity, there is the challenge
of communication; in particular it is a question of tone, of avoiding
mere moaning about 'isms'(e.g. materialism) and of finding imaginative and positive ways of presenting the Christian vision today.

Thirdly, there is the challenge of renewed and genuine community:
this would require a major change in the role of the laity in Church
life.

Fourthly, there is what can be called an option for options: how to
steer the transition from an accustomed level of Church-reliant faith
to a faith more alert and critical within the real world of today?

The last two challenges can be viewed in the light of two moments in Luke's gospel that come significantly side by side. In chapter ten, immediately after the parable of the Good Samaritan, comes the episode of Martha and Mary. The parable counsels imaginative action to look into the ditches, to cross the road and to help the wounded. But Martha is not supported in her activism; instead Mary is praised for her quiet listening to Jesus. Thus the two moments contradict one another, and perhaps with a purpose: the relationship of the believer to transforming this world is more active than the wavelength of a contemplative encounter with God. But the two are profoundly linked and they point to the two final challenges to Irish religion now.

The fifth challenge is the need for spiritual depth: nothing is more likely to foster roots in faith than learning to pray personally and nothing is more likely to cause disillusionment with church life than neglect of people's hunger for 'an awareness of God's presence in the secularised world in which they live' (Bishop Murray).

Finally, there is the challenge of building real bridges between our traditional faith and a new justice-conscience. Is this not the litmus test of the Gospel itself? When John the Baptist ran into doubts in his dark prison and sent messenger to Jesus to ask if he really were the One who was promised, the answer was extremely simple: look at the fruits, people are being set free, and the poor are finding good news.

Notes:
1. Statistics in this paragraph are drawn from Ann Breslin and John Weafer, *Religious Beliefs, Practice and Moral Attitudes: A Comparison of Two Irish Surveys 1974-1984*, (Council of Research and Development), 1985.
2. Máire Nic Ghiolla Phádraig, 'Religious Practice and Secularization', in *Ireland: a Sociological Profile*, ed Patrick Clancy et al, Dublin, IPA, 1986, p. 149.
3. Donal Murray, *The Future of the Faith: Atheism, Non-Belief and Religious Indifference in Ireland*, Dublin, Veritas, 1985, p.7.
4. Liam Ryan, 'The Task of the Church', *The Tablet*, 16th March 1985, p. 275.
5. James Fowler, *Stages of Faith: The Psychology of Human Development and the Quest for Meaning*, New York, Harper and Row, 1981.
6. Juan Luis Segundo, *Hidden Motives of Pastoral Action*, New York, Orbis, 1978. Quotations here are from pp. 48, 34, 131.

An Optimist-Pessimist Dialogue

A young medical student from Australia, on a two-months' visit to Ireland, concluded he could not be a Catholic in Ireland. At home in Melbourne, Paul is a committed Catholic, and so his unsolicited impressions on the Church here seem all the more interesting. He has been to many places throughout Ireland, staying with a usefully distributed network of cousins, and glimpsing the religious situations as he travelled. 'Why this conclusion?' I asked.

'There is no nourishment in what is offered.'

'In what sense?'

'The tone of many sermons is close to fire-and-brimstone, or at least to putting people down.'

'But why are the churches so full?'

'It must be fear, or habit; besides you don't see so many of my generation, and I don't blame them.'

Listening to Paul reminded me that for most of the younger generation in Ireland the image of the Church seems to be poor. Even if I want to point to signs of hope – as I do – I have to admit that on the whole the situaion is not healthy. It is often as Paul describes. Disappointment is more common than anger. Confusion is more usual than outright rejection. But then disappointment and confusion seem strongly present in the young Irish at the moment. In a country with the highest proportion of young adults in Europe, employment prospects are bleak even for university graduates and practically nonexistent for the poor or unskilled. Emigration is back to high levels – of about one hundred young people a day. The present government has managed to plug into a certain puritan righteousness whereby we are now doing penance for our economic recklessness of recent decades (overborrowing to continue the boom of the 1960's into the deception of the 1970's). It is hardly surprising that this more general depression should percolate into the religious scene as well.

Other factors have had their impact too. For a few decades now Ireland has been undergoing a slow but perceptible secularisation. The social changes that began in the late 1950's meant the gradual death of an older more rural-based culture of obedience and the arrival of a more cosmopolitan culture of experience. Whereas previously authority (of all kinds) seemed to hold unquestioned sway, the 1960's opened many doors of freedom, but also of rootlessness. More than other parts of Ireland, the increasingly urbanised east coast (where British television could be received) showed signs of moving from older anchors into a stage of cultural confusion. It would be naïve to scapegoat these external forces as foreign kidnappers of Celtic spirituality.

Ireland in these years made a conscious option to give priority to economics and to enter the European Common Market.

In retrospect, it now seems clear that, in this rapidly changing situation, the communicating Church lacked pastoral imagination and tended to speak an older language. Thus the religious attitudes of young people evolved from the alienation of the 1960's through the anger of the 1970's to the dominant apathy of the 1980's. The object of that apathy is not God, or religion as such, but the Church and its perceived life of practices, preachings and moralities – as my friend Paul discerned. Perhaps in many ways this is a familiar story, in no way limited to this island. Throughout Church history the Gospel has needed liberation from the reductiveness of religion, especially when that religion seemed strongly established. Church life is experienced as complacent or empty while all around a new culture creates an environment alien to any commitment.

A fascinating set of figures shows that strong unbelievers, although still a tiny minority, are increasing by leaps and bounds over the last few decades. The national census returns reveal a dramatic rise in the numbers of those categorising themselves as of 'No religion'; in 1961 one person in 2,546; in 1971 one person in 391; in 1981 one person in 87. And we are not far from 1991. It tempts one to adapt the famous line of Yeats and to claim: 'Catholic Ireland's dead and gone, it's with de Valera in the grave.' As always, the truth is more complicated.

Other authors, if invited to write this short report, would no doubt concentrate on the news headlines of recent years. They would discuss the significance of the two national referendums in which the Church seemed to win by substantial majorities – forbidding abortion by writing it into the Constitution and refusing to remove a prohibition on civil divorce from the 1937 Constitution. They would also write about the appointment of conservative and/ or academic bishops. This writer is somewhat dubious about those headlines as representing where the action is, and indeed increasingly suspicious of the liberal and disdainful-toward-church stance of the media in general. An intelligent public discussion of religion is rare either in Irish newspapers or on radio and television. Controversy about religious issues is preferred, and hence the level remains immature and vaguely adolescent in its rebelliousness. This might not be an inaccurate guage of where many of our university graduates are in terms of faith maturity. It is a scandal that in the university founded by Cardinal Newman, theology is forbidden by how we interpret an old British law, and thus generations of students graduate as religious illiterates. Newman must be dizzy in his grave. In line with this, our major newspapers practically never print reviews of religious books. In this predominantly religious country, intellectual malnutrition reaches epidemic proportions as many adults go through lives of faithful church practice on the meagre mental diet assimilated in high school.

That dangerous level of intellectual undernourishment has been honestly recognised by the bishops themselves. Indeed, some excellent pastoral letters in recent years have drawn attention to various areas of crisis within Irish Catholicism. One such text spoke of many people 'going through adult lives with ideas about religion more suitable for primary schoolboys and schoolgirls.' Another questioned whether 'our concept of religion gives proper place to justice and charity as well as to Mass and the sacraments.' Still another pastoral letter faced the special difficulties of young people over 'a Church that doesn't seem to offer a genuine community.' In the light of these statements, one might say that there is a fairly clear recognition at an official level that the Irish Catholic Church is far from having found its language for the new Ireland that has emerged from the previously rural and sheltered situation.

One could summarise the challenge as involving four areas of crisis. The first is the transition from a passive church membership to an experience of the local parish as fostering involvement and growth. The second would mean moving from practice to praxis, in the sense of a faith much more conscious of itself as called to change history through a struggle for justice. The third need has to do with personal faith development, with moving from convention to conviction, and especially with finding some deeper wavelength of Scripture reading and of personal prayer. The fourth area has already been mentioned as the educational or intellectual need for a firmer grasp of the meaning of faith, one that can survive honestly within a more complex culture.

These challenges have been recognised and in many places are being responded to. Unless they are tackled even more urgently, Irish Catholicism could become culturally marginal even while preserving impressive external adherence. The normal values might continue to seem Christian, but the operative values in Irish society would be increasingly acculturated to the dominant secularism of Europe.

The previous paragraphs constitute what can be called a majority report, and it has inevitably been a recital of problems and difficulties. But there is also another story to be told of positive achievements and signs of hope alive in Ireland now. A minority report for these last few years can be much more optimistic. In fact, adult education courses in religion are a significant success story in practically every county in Ireland – and often with a high level of commitment involving one night a week over a period of two years. Similarly, there are exciting new developments in youth ministry. Every Saturday evening, the Mass in the back chapel of the pro-Cathedral of Dublin is crowded with young people. It was inspired by the successful work with European youth of the Taizé monastery in the south of France. Likewise an old convent in Tullow, called *Teach Bríde* or House of Bridget, has become an experimental open house where young adults can reflect on issues of faith in a contemplative and friendly atmosphere. This centre is run by one diocesan priest with a team of young lay people. Within second-level education, many schools in recent years have begun to employ trained lay catechists (graduates of Mater Dei Institute in Dublin or Mount Oliver in Dundalk): these are often much better equipped to communicate the faith to contemporary young people in the classroom than some of the older religious working in the schools (As the years go on, fewer and fewer religious are available for secondary education). The retreat movement, previously the preserve of religious, has begun to reach out into parishes, and often into poorer areas, offering training in prayer and in spiritual direction for ordinary people – and with extraordinary success.

Similarly, a sensitivity to justice issues has become the special thrust of many religious, women and men; and linked with them is a whole network of socially alert young people often influenced by the liberation spirituality of Latin America. Even in the shadow of the Northern Ireland conflict, ecumenism has made remarkable advances in some places and at the local level.

Small is beautiful – at least let us hope so. None of these developments is more than a pocket of wisdom, but they are evidence of an exciting, if minority, aliveness within Irish Catholicism now. The point is that the headlines and the statistics are not the whole story. Religion in Ireland is at a crucial moment in its history. There is much to worry about. Equally there is much to be grateful for.

The truth about the Irish religious situation cannot avoid being a double message. Yes, religion is still uniquely important here, with deep roots in families, with impressive presence in education, with those extraordinary levels of practice, and so on. And yet what does it all mean? Has it any clout (as we would say) to turn the Republic of Ireland from becoming an egoist and competitive society where a comfortable middle class cares little for the one-fourth and more of the population living in poverty? Have we passed the point of any national consensus about basic goals and values? Are we going to listen to the anger of the prophets in our midst? To Francis Stuart, our most distinguished living novelist, for instance: 'If Irish Catholicism is to become something more than an utterly bastardised version of the gospels, then it will be through the intensely obsessed and dreaming minds of a comparatively few people and despite most of our church leaders.' Or will we drift with the pop culture tides and vegetate before our televisions, absorbing a philosophy more alien to Christian faith than any overt atheism or communism?

Ireland is a small place with its own strange history. At the beginning of this century it emerged (three-quarters of it at least) painfully into nationhood. As the century begins to end, Ireland is again uncertain about identity and vision. The spiritual strand in Irish culture is still deep, but it is not clear what role it will play in shaping future directions. It could retreat cautiously into the private sphere even while retaining a majority allegiance. Or it could become an imaginative voice to challenge the inhabitants of this island to recognise the drifting nature of our modernity, to resist our negative self-images and so to seize some choices while we can.

From Fate to Choice

Once upon a time in village of Ars, when Saint Jean de Vianney was parish priest, a travelling fiddler came on his rounds. His music kept the people dancing late into the night but the holy man remained dubious as to the moral impact on his flock. So the good Curé approached the fiddler privately and paid him to move on to the next village.

In the fifties in Ireland it was possible to pay the fiddler to move on, or even to ban his arrival in the first place. By the nineties, it is clear that the fiddler of modernity is here to stay and that the younger generations will usually dance to whatever tune the fiddler plays. That is perhaps the crux of Ireland's new situation for faith.

The story of these decades of change is relatively familiar. Up to the fifties Catholicism in Ireland moved within a simple model of life, a village consensus, where religion naturally dominated without necessarily domineering. Catholicism and culture walked hand in hand (at least in the South). The Catholicism of those times, as in other parts of the world, was pious but passive, and neither of those characteristics prepared it for the double shock of the sixties – the social changes born from the new economics and the church changes born from the Council. New wealth brought new life-styles and a population shift towards the urbanised east. Thus Ireland came to echo, in its own slow way, the process often observed in other countries: that where older forms of community are rocked, attitudes go into confusion. To borrow a phrase from the sociologist Peter Berger, when a traditional culture is confronted with modernity, people move 'from fate to choice', from life as shaped by inherited ways to the burden of decision – or else to the non-decision of drift.

Is there a major crisis of faith in Ireland? Many would say yes and point to the decline in Mass attendance among sections of the population as an obvious signal of that crisis. But does that undoubted fall-off in practice, particularly among the young, constitute a 'crisis of faith'? It seems better to describe it as a crisis in the language of faith, or in the language of Church. The trouble lies not in the core of the creed but in how it is experienced or communicated or lived. I know quite a few young adults who struggle to retain some scaffolding of prayer or other ways of nourishing their somewhat private faith, but who have opted out of their parents' principal language of faith which put so central a stress on Sunday Mass-going.

Four Types of Youth

My more than twenty years of teaching literature at the largest state university suggests that for most of that time the proportions of reaction to religion among young people (students and non-students) have not greatly altered. There seem to be four distinguishable groupings. On the positive wing, there are those who remain active and involved in Church activities. These range from enthusiastic members of folk-groups to organisers of social awareness programmes, for instance 'urban plunge', whereby teenagers of different social classes visit one another as part of a raising of consciousness about social divisions. Some students opt for special training as catechists or youth ministers (and opportunities for jobs in this direction are increasing). Others seek out ways of spirituality and deeper lives of prayer. This committed group of searchers and builders might represent about 10% of students and young people in general.

On the opposite wing are those who have become openly embittered and hostile to the Catholicism of their upbringing. These young unbelievers would be strongly critical of the hypocrisy of the church institution as they perceive it. Although they might not represent more than another 10%, their voices make themselves heard and they often end up in high-profile positions in the media or public life.

A large majority lies in the middle and divides into two more or less equal groups, those who mainly opt in to church belonging and those who mainly opt out. The exact line between these two is not easy to discern but it is certainly a new phenomenon in post-modernised Ireland. A significant gap is opening between those for whom Catholicism remains a spiritual home, a place of roots however shaky, and those who feel themselves in more awkward and distant relationship with their inherited religion. These latter, who opt out, tend now to do so quietly, without anger, even without major parental fights. They simply drop any regular Sunday practice and remain cultural Catholics without the props of the older unified culture that their parents knew. They live therefore with a tenuous and insecure connection with the Church. This pattern of distancing from practice would be much more noticeable in urban areas than in rural.

The other half of the majority in the middle constitutes the main group of young people regularly at Sunday Mass (and Ireland's statistics here here would be higher than any other country in Europe). Unlike the minority of the actively committed, these seldom have any other public involvement of a religious kind except this fidelity to Sunday attendance. They remain faithful to it for many reasons, sometimes because of happy roots in a believing family, sometimes because they experience spiritual nourishment through their Sunday observance. But that nourishment is of such a minimum kind that in the long run this important group runs the risk of malnutrition. It is true that some of them go further in a positive direction and frequent special occasions that have proved popular in recent years. One thinks of penance services or pilgrimages to Lough Derg or Taizé, or helping out with holidays for handicapped. Many of this crucial group seem impressed by the active stance of church people dedicated to working with the deprived, whether at home or abroad.

New Prophetic Voice

That brings me to a piece of good news which could not have been offered with the same confidence in any previous year. There has been an avalanche of comment concerning the more vocal and committed social stance of many of the Catholic bishops within the last year or so. A recent and much-publicised front page of the popular *Sunday Press* began its cover story: 'The Catholic Church has become an outspoken champion of the rights of the poor ... has the Church truly become the main Opposition?' Another distinguished journalist expressed her comic embarrassment as an ex-Catholic in finding herself so often in agreement with the Church's criticism of the government's economic policies. 'Week after week', wrote Mary Holland, 'it is the Conference of Major Religious Superiors which lays out with devastating clarity the political choices which face the government and warns of the consequences if it fails to take the radical action necessary to improve the lot of the poor.' Archbishop Cassidy of Tuam attracted considerable attention when he expressed his hope for 1989 that 'there would be a growing sense of national outrage that any family would be famished for food' adding that unless we are 'outraged by inequality, nothing will change'. This is hardly a new Catholic stance in itself; what is significant is that with increasing strength this note within the chord of faith is being sounded at official Church level, being heard much more widely than before, and even being responded to at government level in some of their budget choices.

This social emphasis presents an attractive face of the Church for many of the young and uncertain believers, but it seems significant in a larger sense. It marks a new confidence within the Irish Catholic Church after years of sensing itself to be losing credibility in the eyes of the emerging culture. The fiddler of modernity seemed to have all the best tunes and to have the under thirties totally in thrall. As a result, for a decade or more, the Church has felt somewhat on the defensive in the struggle of images that is so central in this television age. Often the Church has been perceived as dull, boring, unalive and cautious. What many young people experienced in worship only confirmed this negative image in the media. Although the Church was usually thought of as a powerful influence in Irish society, in fact it was becoming a weak partner in the battle of 'image-ology' over what life is about. Besides, with the break-up of the old community consensus of rural Ireland, the agenda of religion had tended to narrow into the individualistic and the purely personal. The outcome was that the official Church has seemed strangely oppressed and confused by the secularising and privatising culture around it until it discovered anew its more prophetic voice on social issues.

In O'Casey's old masterpiece, *The Plough and the Stars,* the first major laugh goes to a line of Fluther's: 'I think we ought to have as great a regard for religion as we can, so as to keep it out of as many things as possible'. The Fluther philosophy has been a sadly strong strand in Irish Catholicism: hang on to the externals and don't think too much. But with the pressures of the new culture and with the upheavals of so much social change, it is clear that such a formula is a recipe for practical atheism or at least for a shallow and unworthy adherence. In Irish usage 'faith' is not the same as 'the faith': the latter expression points to traditions of practice and the former more to the decision over a way of Christian life 'The faith' was the pride of an older Ireland. 'Faith' is more the need of today. If both are endangered in new ways, they are also coming alive in new ways. The shift from fate to choice has not been easy, but instead of trying to ban the fiddler of modernity, the Church is discovering herself able, at times, to provide an alert and alternative music. And many are still listening.

PART TWO : Christianity and Modern Culture

The only room that secular culture reserves for religion is within the subjectivity of the private individual.
Wolfgang Pannenberg, 1988

Less specifically Irish in focus than in the first part, the pieces gathered here examine some of the struggles of faith peculiar within modernity. Is apathy the dominant mood of now? What do we understand by secularisation? How can a believer understand his or her atheist friends, and respond to them with reverence? Is faith merely a product of imagination? What is happening in the area of faith ministry to youth? What are the changing tones of belief and unbelief within recent years?

An Anatomy of Religious Indifference

The graffitist who signed 'God' after the statement 'Nietzsche is dead' captured something of the religious situation of the seventies. A quarter of a century ago Karl Rahner wrote an eloquent analysis of 'anguished atheism'[1] but that phenomenon has almost entirely disappeared from the contemporay horizon. We moved on to the secularisation talk of the honest-to-God controversies of the early sixties and then, to everyone's surprise, to the arrival of the Jesus movement and the explosion of interest in the occult in the seventies.

Clearly these trends do not mean the return of religious faith; indeed they can be interpreted as a revival of idolatry – of that more virulent unbelief, much more ancient than the various atheisms that have resulted from upheavals in ideas and society for some two centuries now. Just as the Jesus movement could be the consumer society's package deal, cashing in on frustrated religiousness, so the more recent occultism could be a deeper stage of the same neo-paganism. And meanwhile, beneath the froth of these minority tendencies, the fate of faith seemed to be changing radically: in the so-called developed world, the religious crisis of recent years has been less one of explicit atheism than of sheer indifference on a massive scale, and of the falling away from faith by many previous adherents.

If Nietzsche is dead, in this sense, then who is alive? Perhaps Kierkegaard's 'aesthetic man', the person who drifts with the tide, who lacks selfhood and makes no real choices.

A significant pointer for the Catholic Church in this respect was the publication in 1978 of a volume of specialist essays on religious indifference by the Vatican Secretariat for Non-Believers – the first time in their fifteen years of existence that they gave any prominence to the topic.[2] And our purpose here is to study indifference as the majority version of unbelief today in the western world. The examination will fall into three sections, tackling these questions: indifference to what? from where? so what? Thus the first part will deal with types, the second with causes, and the third with responses.

Indifferent to What?

Religious indifference... is the least conspicuous form of atheism: it has hardly any expression on the doctrinal level, and on the practical level it rarely takes militant or aggressive forms, so that one is tempted to pay it less attention. It is, however, ... the most radical form of atheism; it challenges not only the existence of God and the possibility of knowing him, but the very consistency of the religious problem. Nowhere is the absence of God so total.[3]

This statement from Jules Girardi offers a usefully strong expression of the nature of indifference. Similarly the Second Vatican Council had described it in terms of a deadening of the religious question:

Some never get to the point of raising questions about God, since they seem to experience no religious stirrings nor do they see why they should trouble themselves about religion (*GS* 19).

But even this one sentence suggests two very different types of indifference: a radical ignoring of any religious search or wondering, and disinterest in the world of religion – and this (although it is not specified) often means the world of church-mediated religion. Hence at the outset here it is necessary to clarify the various kinds of indifference possible. The term covers not only the strong meaning of closedness to any horizon of transcendence, but also a whole spectrum of what the French would call *distanciation*; where the meaning or value of some component of religion becomes dulled and one finds oneself consciously or unconsciously 'distanced' from any contact with it.

One person may be distant from the sacraments, for example, but not from faith and prayer; another may be distant from any real sense of Christ, but not without religious searching. To answer our question – indifferent to what? – one may draw on the eight kinds of 'progressive distanciation' listed by André Charron in 1975 as part of his research for the Montreal Service *Incroyance et Foi*, the Canadian Secretariat for non-Believers.[4] According to Charron the following is a possible pattern of how people move from non-practice or indifference to the worship dimensions of faith through various or increasingly serious withdrawal until they finally reach a state of complete indifference:

1) distance from liturgical practice;

2) from the Church as institution; this would include active and passive marginals depending on whether they have definite objections to the Church or simply drift with a secularised society;

3) from the Church as community of believers; this would cover sociological or nominal believers and non-adherents who have cut their links more clearly;

4) from Christian practice, where there is no influence of belief on behaviour;

5) from the synthesis of Christian meaning, involving some rejection (a) of Church teaching or (b) of the Gospel itself;

6) from adherence in faith to Jesus Christ, this being the point in the process of 'distanciation' where one arrives at post-Christian unbelief in the strict sense;

7) distance from faith in a personal God – either agnostic or atheistic;

8) from all religious questioning – hence religious indifference in

its fullest sense of a complete absence of interest in the possibility of faith.

In the light of this scheme one could speak of two polarities within the spectrum of various kinds of indifference: the earlier stages above could be termed the 'alienation' pole and later stages the 'apathy' pole, in the sense that, what begins as disappointment with the externals of Church life, and a certain disengagement from involvement, can become, in time, a more closed and impenetrable state of disinterest in all matters of faith. If external religious practice has played a central role as an expression of commitment, its abandonment will leave a great void. Research in Canada has strongly questioned the optimistic hypothesis that faith can often continue in individuals despite diminution of their religious practice; while this may be true for a minority of conscientious searchers, the abandonment of a pattern of practice by the majority will almost certainly reveal a lack of commmitment, and, in a situation of pluralism, indifference to practice can quickly evolve into an eclipse of faith itself.

Psychological research, also connected with the Montreal Secretariat, would suggest that what we have been calling the 'alienation' and 'apathy' polarities within religious indifference are differentiated by being before or after a stage of 'anger' or hostility.[5] According to this line of thinking, an early stage of indifference takes the form of frustration due to passivity and dependence: one is involved in the routines of church-going but in such a way that they remain meaningless and the person is left feeling dissatisfied and distant. This can erupt into rebellion against the pattern in a phase of hostility, which in turn opens the way for a third stage of cold separation, apathy, indifference. This latter form, which is the aftermath of anger, is a more deeply rooted distancing of oneself from the religious horizon than the earlier stage of disinterest in practice. But the progression from initial to fuller types of indifference is relatively easy, and hence one should not be dismissive of the pastoral seriousness of abandonment of Mass-going. To quote André Charron again:

> The abandonment of liturgical practice can lead to the numbing of Christian practice, that is to say of a faith alive in deeds, if not to the loss of this faith in the long term through distance.... from any community support, from any pedagogy in the meeting with God, with his Word, and with the sacraments. [6]

This account of indifference has stressed its manifold nature and at the same time the progressive relationship between its various kinds. In all its senses it stands for the opposite to strong and clear commitment in some direction and thus it is quite different from energetic atheism and energetic faith alike. Indeed it may be more easily described in negative rather than in positive terms: it is not a matter of ideas or of the denial of the existence of God as a doctrine – much more a matter of a state of mind or attitude that experiences religion as irrelevant. Indifference involves a double absence – of religion from human reality today and of people from religious reality. Having offered this sketch of what indifference entails, one can now ask why this form of unbelief has come to be so crucial in our generation.

The Causes of Indifference Today

In the previous section we saw that abandonment of worship or religious practice may be a significant first step in the process of becoming 'distanced' from the reality of personal faith (and that this is especially true against a background of large-scale conventional adherence to religion as in Ireland). Putting this in different language, one may say that indifference may begin as a crisis of Church mediations but end as a crisis of religious consciousness. What starts as an understandable carelessness can continue until it finds that the whole horizon of faith becomes massively unreal. But what makes this massive unreality so uniquely possible today?

Our hypothesis here is that indifference is the product of a convergence of different factors. Indeed, just as Newman liked to present assent to faith not as a matter of logic but as a complex convergence of positive evidence, so one might speak of indifference as connected with various negative convergences. Indifference is a passive happening, a non-decision rather than a choice, and as such it may be understood as the product of a four-fold convergence of factors in modern life: (a) the deadening of the religious search through the sheer impetus of social change; (b) the failure of the mediations of religion to meet and speak with the culture of today; (c) the humanist context of values where the notion of God seems alien or embarrassing to the mind; (d) the filtering down of the arguments of great atheist thinkers into more popular assumptions. The rest of this section will expand on these points.

What Christ himself, in the parable of the sower, saw as the choking thorns, the distractions of superficial living, is an intensely magnified feature of the modern context. What Pascal called *divertissement*, protecting people from both boredom and truth, shows itself in immensely more complex forms today. T.S. Eliot once wrote of contemporary man being 'distracted from distraction by distraction', and certainly many aspects of the amusement society can be seen almost as a conspiracy of superficiality, and hence as a major influence towards indifference. The consumerist life-style keeps mystery at bay and aborts the religious question before it comes to consciousness. It provides alternative sacralisations – sex, sport, security, success – so that the centre of life is subtly but definitely shifted from interiority of faith to the dominance of other values and concerns.

There is no point in bemoaning the presence of television or in lamenting economic development or in hoping to reverse urbanisation. But it is essential to recognise that such factors create a drastically different environment for faith, and one in which indifference can easily evolve through the various stages of 'distanciation' mentioned in the previous section. In short, such rapid social change has spelt the death of conventional religion in so far as it remains merely conventional.

The growing irrelevance of Church activities to people exposed to today's culture is a second major source favourable to indifference. As already mentioned, we are experiencing, not so much a crisis of faith in the pure sense, as a crisis of the mediations of faith. This affects the younger generations more acutely because it is a crisis on the level of experience as an empty duty, a source of shallowness and boredom; and pastors often fall into a 'category mistake' in thinking that a problem on the level of relationship can be solved if only people understand the meaning of the liturgy. It is a problem of mutual communication, and the gaps widen between the world of the everyday and the churchy world. This creates another sure formula for indifference because when I feel myself both unheard and unspoken to over a long period, I can only experience distance and disinterest.

In this situation a serious pastoral discernment is called for if the Church itself is not to contribute to its own marginalisation in the consciousness of those groups already showing signs of collective withdrawal: the young, the urban, the workers, the highly educated. To continue to spend too much energy in servicing the conventional needs of the conventional believer is hardly obedient to the Lord's precept: leave the majority of ninety-nine in the desert and seek out, caringly and creatively, even a minority of one. Perhaps it is a typically Church-centred temptation to invest time and effort in the maintenance of familiar patterns: the good can blind one to the better and to the more pressing and more difficult call. In other words, a Church that seems indifferent to those who begin to feel indifferent can only confirm their indifference.

If the two causes so far mentioned deal with contexts that affect consciousness, the two remaining ones touch more on contents – attitudes and ideas – which at least indirectly promote indifference to religion. They can be examined fairly briefly. Karl Rahner has argued that a 'hominised world implies inevitable distancing of God'[7] or, in Saul Bellow's witty variant on Wordsworth, the world is too much with us and there has never been so much world. The assumptions of modern culture are radically humanist, and these assumptions percolate down even to those who would not know what the term 'humanism' means. The implicit norms of modern work and of modern leisure are often closed to anything spiritual; rationalist and pragmatic ideas are part of the air one breathes. The result is that the religious horizon recedes into what we have described as massive unreality, and that this can be vaguely but 'rationally' understood and justified in terms of a commonsense realism. Once again the door is opened to indifference, this time by the new self-sufficiency of the world.

The last of our four converging causes has to do with the heritage of strongly atheistic philosophies of existence and how these can indirectly create a diminishing plausibility for religion and an increasing risk of indifference. For people moving through the phases of indifference already outlined, ideas are not absent but only unclearly present: they can know, without having worked out, that intellectual rejection of religion is in the air, that a long tradition of critique of faith has been enormously powerful (from Feuerbach to Freud, from Marx to Monod); they will hardly know the great names but they may have picked up the drift second-hand and that is enough to defend their indifference, should defence be called for. A rumour that faith is not credible any more has reached them and rumours are enough to promote a kind of unbelief that feels little need for real decisions or definite affirmations and negations.

One can be surprised at the sheer ignorance of the contents of faith revealed by those drifting from it (when they come to articulate their position at all) and equally by the perhaps incoherent summaries of the great atheists that may have been heard in some television debate and that serve to bolster the incipient indifference. Thus, what for the nineteenth century constituted the God-crisis of a few, can become in the late twentieth century the God-absence of the many.

It may be added that the type of indifference that is envisaged as issuing from the convergence of these four factors is characterised by both passivity and immaturity. This is not to deny that there are other kinds of active and mature indifference, as in the case of the person who has explored the question of God, arrived at negative options, and now lives in a relatively tranquil state of indifference. But this is the exceptional case and we are speaking rather of the majority phenomenon: the passive victim of convergent influences that were too strong to withstand, and the spiritually immature who, in Jung's words, have 'no capacity of discernment for the things of the inner world'.[8]

Possibilities of Pastoral Response

In 1817 de Lamennais wrote a celebrated *Essai sur l'indifférence en matier de religion,* claiming that 'the sickest century is not that which becomes impassioned for error,but the century which neglects and scorns the truth'.[9] The types of indifference envisaged here, however, do not call for such impassioned judgment; they are not of this totally closed kind which de Lamennais had in mind; our typical case is rather of someone moving through the 'progressive distanciation' studied by André Charron in the Quebec situation. Our background is Britain and Ireland rather than France, and hence we are not thinking of that deeply engrained indifference inherited through generations, but one that is more the outcome of a relatively recent crisis of culture, leading to decline in religious coherence and belonging. In the Irish or British situation one can assume that the vast majority of Catholics endangered by various levels of indifference were at least brought up as believers, probably experienced periods of fervour, and hence their roots in faith are not forgotten even though its meaning and present expression seem in doubt.

The previous two sections belong to pastoral theology in that they tried to understand the issues raised by indifference. But when one asks our third question, about responses to this problem, answers are not easy to find. The very nature of religious indifference poses a double problem for pastoral action: how to enter into contact at all, and how to create willingness to be contacted on the part of the indifferent. Our suggestions here are sketchy and tentative, and they fall into two categories. First, we shall examine some general principles of apostolate in this area, and secondly, we shall raise a number of practical possibilities.

Even for those more deeply imbued with disinterest in religious matters, the Second Vatican Council held that their indifference could not be a total life stance:

Man is constantly worked upon by God's Spirit, and hence can never be altogether indifferent to the problem of religion ... man will always yearn to know, at least in an obscure way, what is the meaning of his life, of his activity, of his death (*GS* 41).

It follows from this that a fundamental pastoral strategy would be to seek out the special moments when indifference becomes aware of its own inadequacy, and when people may be grateful for the opportunity to listen to the questions that surface for them. This first principle, then, refers to privileged threshold moments as potentially fruitful. The problem, as we shall see, is how to recognise them and how to enter into contact with people at those times.

A second principle refers to basic pastoral attitudes towards the indifferent or the half-believing, and one can draw here on some suggestions of Karl Rahner. With his typical de-emphasising of the explicit statements of faith and his special focus on the already-present and implicit grace within each individual, Rahner likes to insist that every apostolate is an uncovering of what is hidden within people's hearts:

The grace of God has always been there ahead of our preaching ... Hence our preaching is not really an indoctrination with something alien from outside but the awakening of something within, as yet not understood but nevertheless really present.

A corollary of this in Rahner's thinking is what he calls the strategy of 'mystagogy', which would seek to 'describe and focus the attention of each individual in his concrete existence on those experiences in which he in his individuality had the experience of transcendence and of being taken up out of himself'.[10] Translating this into a different vocabulary, one could say that mystagogy means discerning and disclosing the mysteries within each person's life-story; as such it would communicate to the indifferent, not primarily in terms of God and faith, but in terms of their own experiences of self-transcendence and struggle, with the confidence that within these experiences the presence of God can be unveiled.

A third general principle may be borrowed from the more concrete and psychological research of Léopold de Reyès of the Montreal Service *Incroyance et Foi*, and it would consist of a warning against frequently unhelpful ways of communication by believers towards the indifferent. Using the vocabulary of 'transactional analysis', de Reyes has demonstrated how often the lapsed or 'distanced' experience believers as excessively rigid and authoritarian ('Parent'), excessively manipulating and coldly intellectual ('Adult'), and either aggressive or naïvely sentimental ('Child') in their presentations of their faith.[11] The positive thesis to emerge from this investigation is that in any attempted dialogue the relationship is much more important than the content, and that only a relationship of mutual freedom and respect as equals (what is embodied in the slogan 'I'm OK - You're OK') can lead to fruitful interaction between believer and someone involved in the spectrum of *distanciation*.

Conclusion

People today seldom 'lose the faith' by conscious rejection but rather by their images of God ceasing to inform their lives. Hence, religious indifference, in manifold forms, seems to be the most quietly sinister threat to faith now. Any pastoral response to it must include two large fronts: an uphill struggle against the pollutions of consciousness that endanger western life, and the slow service of the entire inner renewal of the Church. Of course, this latter heading raises a vast number of questions: how to deepen the spiritual and

intellectual dimensions of faith? at the same time, how to educate believers away from a narrowly private version of faith and towards
awareness and service of justice? how to build a flexible variety of sup-
port-communities for faith – since so many aspects of Christian life
are left undernourished by an exclusive emphasis on church-going?
how to insure that a true image of God is communicated – since impoverished images, such as the deist clock-maker or the moral tyrant,
are sure breeding grounds for indifference.

The struggle for faith has changed its ground significantly in the
years since the Council – from being thought of primarily in doctrinal
and institutional terms as a countering of atheism, to being a pastoral
and cultural crisis of religious indifference. Faced with this situation,
it is imperative that faith be a conviction rather than a convention,
that the crucial decision of faith be rooted in a person's experience
and also find support through shared reflection and shared commitment with others. In short, both to recognise and to respond to the
many faces of indifference would seem to constitute one of the greatest challenges to pastoral theology today.

Notes:

1. 'Science as a Confession', *Theological Investigations,* iii,1967,
385ff.
2. *L'Indifferenza Religiosa,* ed. Vincenzo Miano, Rome, 1978.
3. 'Reflections on Religious Indifference', *Concilium,* iii, (Mar
1967), 31.
4. A. Charron, 'Les Divers Types de Distants', *Nouveau Dialogue*
No. 11, (April 1975), 3-9.
5. Léopold de Reyès,'Diverses phases du processus de conversion',
Nouveau Dialogue, No. 29 (March 1979), 30-34.
6. *Une Pratique Dominicale et Chrétienne a Redecouvrir,* Montreal,
1975, p. 19
7. 'The Man of Today and Religion', *Theological Investigations,* vi,
11.
8. Cited in *L'Indifferenza Religiosa,* p.77.
9. Ibid., p.9.
10. Rahner, 'On the Significance in Redemptive History of the Individual Member of the Church', *Mission and Grace,* i, 1963, 156.
11. 'L'Interlocuteur souhaité par les distants', *Nouveau Dialogue* No.
17 (November 1976), 3-8.

Secularisation and New Forms of Faith

And we forget, because we are leading this modern life,
until we are reminded.
Patrick White

In 1945 T.S. Eliot commented that there was much talk about the 'decline of religious belief' but that, in his view as a poet, the more profound crisis lay in the area of religious feeling:

> The trouble of the modern age is not merely the inability to believe certain things about God which our forefathers believed, but the inability to feel towards God and man as they did. [1]

This secularising of feelings entails a more serious impoverishment than loss of religious practices or confusion over religious truths. It is good to recall this deeper level at the outset. As will be seen, there are many descriptions on offer as to the nature of secularisation: in so far as 'Christianity is communal before being individual',[2] it will appear as a crisis of culture; in so far as the crisis occurs within the religious consciousness of individuals, its core is rather the 'decline of religious sensibility' as pinpointed by Eliot.

If Eliot reminds us that the debate must touch on feelings as distinct from beliefs, a second light from literature can be found in a somewhat unexpected quarter. The philosopher Alasdair MacIntyre has long pondered the issues of secularisation and in his book, *After Virtue*, gives pride of place to – of all people – Jane Austen as 'the last great effective imaginative voice' of the Aristotelian tradition of ethical thought which he is seeking to renew for modern times. He points to a major difference between the modern secular self, for whom value judgements are 'emotivist' expressions of preference, and a more ancient understanding of 'virtue' where the self belonged within a rational context of values.[3] In this Aristotelian tradition, moral judgments are measured against norms larger than the self, but when 'emotivism' takes over, 'I feel like it' or 'I don't feel like it' can become dangerously common yardsticks for serious decisions.

A Fictional View of Crisis

But why should MacIntyre single out Austen as a major exemplar of the transition from more grounded to more subjective moralities? This is not the Austen innocently thought to be a genteel satirist of manners. This is rather the Austen recognised by commentators such as Lionel Trilling as a moralist who presents a subtle challenge to secularist assumptions. In particular she is forever contrasting two types: more urbanised and secular personalities, and those struggling for self-knowledge, but beset by self-deception. Within the seemingly mild pages of Austen's fiction lurks a subversively acute discernment of two ways of life. The emerging secularist culture is portrayed as attractive, lively, sincere, but adrift. The retreating culture is more rooted and rational in its 'disposition' (a key word for Austen) and in many ways her central question can be expressed as: how is non-secularist consciousness to survive within a secularist world?

The value-conflicts of Austen's stories offer an essential reminder that we are talking about experiences rather than interpretations, people rather than 'isms', and that at the heart of the struggle of faith lies the drama of personal choice within a changing culture.

A Collage of Commentators

The tendency of literature to give a privileged status to the personal will find its counterbalance in the tendency of most commentators on secularisation to stress the social factors. Over twenty years ago, the same Alasdair MacIntyre insisted that the key to the secularisation of Britain lay in the 'destruction of older forms of community'[4] by urbanisation, industrialisation and social complexity. In his view 'unbelief in Christianity' does not precede or produce moral change; on the contrary, he would put all the emphasis on the disappearance of social stability as the source of any upheaval of beliefs and values. In this light, our central question here will be: granted that social change has a huge influence on religious attitudes, and granted also that such change is usually irreversible in direction, what forms of faith can survive and even flourish in an inevitably more complex environment?

Before attempting any answers to that question, it is necessary to gather some further clarifications as to the nature of secularisation. According to a common sense view of things, it may be described as a process whereby both organised religion and a sense of mystery decrease in influence during a period of cultural change – change due to an explosion of rational achievements in the ordering of life. But it is well to flesh out that simple approach with something of a collage of diverse commentators, and only then will we be able to single out what seems to be the key to the profile of faith possible in a more secular culture.

It is obvious that 'secularisation' is an umbrella term for a situation produced by the converging of many familiar ingredients: a market economy, industrial urbanisation, technological thinking, an awareness explosion through travel and new media. What had been a fairly unified worldview becomes scattered, pluralist, unsure of its bearings. It all adds up to a post-rural rhythm of life with a resultant relativising of the traditional authorities in many spheres.

Against this general background some commentators put the emphasis on the liberation of areas of influence from Church control, on the arrival of an accepted autonomy of human values independent of religious faith. In this sense Peter Berger had described secularisation as the process 'in which religion loses its hold on the level both of institutions and of human consciousness'.[5] Other commentators prefer to approach it from the point of view of historical changes, as for instance in Owen Chadwick's account of a 'growing tendency in mankind ... to try to do without religion'.[6] According to Bernard Lonergan the 'absence of God in modern culture' is due to three main influences: an awareness that interpretations of life are all of human origin, an extraordinary transformation of society in recent times, and 'a new sense of power and responsibility'.[7] Antonio Grumelli sees secularisation as stemming from three factors: ideological pluralism, the dominance of functional patterns of thought, and the sophisticated restlessness which is the urbanised life-style.[8] Jane Austen might not like the jargon but would be strangely in tune with the content!

Grumelli is particularly relevant for our present purposes since he explores the extent to which this distancing of society from religious influence can entail large-scale loss of faith. He sees this outcome as more likely where 'a religious outlook was embodied in the cultural components of a society' and where a previously high-profile Church suddenly finds itself in a period of rapid change. In other words, secularisation is an endangering force principally for a superficially sociological religion, or in so far as either belief or unbelief may be a 'function of the social environment'. Grumelli sums up his optimistic hypothesis about the purifying potentials as follows:

> Like the process of rationality, secularisation can be fertile ground for atheism; but by the same token, it can bring about religious growth and maturity... it can also stimulate new religious concern, eliciting the reaction of deeper, autonomous, internalised, and mature religious adherence.[9]

Ambiguity of Responses

What is emerging is that secularisation can be quite diverse in its impact on religious patterns and attitudes and hence one finds the more theological commentators ambivalent in their responses to it. Sometimes they see it as a welcome new world where the Church can be more unburdened and free in its witness to Christ; alternatively they view it as a dangerous moment where many people can fall victim to a prevailing confusion of values and may ultimately lose contact with their religious roots and needs. What is clear is that the arrival of a more secular culture need not spell the sudden demise of religion as such, but it does constitute a severe challenge to the embodiments and languages of religion. It brings about not so much a crisis of faith as of the languages of faith. In particular the institutional embodiments of worship, which may have served a more stable culture well, can simply fail to meet the spiritual needs of a generation shaped by mobility of culture. This point is put with energy by Langdon Gilkey:

> Forms of religion developed in another cultural epoch and enshrining their religious ideas, norms, and roles in the shapes of that past cultural existence can become, when historical changes occur, anachronistic, oppressive, even possibly demonic, and certainly irrelevant in the new age. [10]

Implicit in much of the argument so far is one major insight about the kind of faith that can come to maturity in a more secular setting. It is a faith that can cope with the burden of choice. A more secularised culture offers a radically expanded menu of life-styles. One has only to think of the typical contrast between village and city to realise that the anonymity of the urban allows for a much wider set of moralities in practice than would the smaller pressures of the village world. Sociologists and theologians alike seem to be agreed on this point – that secularisation inaugurates a different horizon where choices must be made if people are not to fall into a passivity of drifting with the tide.

Thus in the late sixties, Peter Berger showed how the 'plausibility' of faith begins to run into trouble in any more open environment than it has been accustomed to – even to the extent that 'the dynamics of consumer preference are introduced into the religious sphere'.[11] In a more recent book, he has described modernity as the 'near inconceivable expansion of the area of human life open to choices'.[12] This same emphasis on choice can be found in the more theological writings of Karl Rahner as early as the fifties. We have entered, in his opinion, into a period that is 'irreversibly secularised' and the crucial change for faith lies in the'conditions surrounding human decision'. Rahner returned to this theme at the opening of his final major work, where he evoked without nostalgia the situation of his own youth when a faith milieu was taken for granted:

> Our faith was partially and essentially conditioned by a quite different sociological situation which at that time supported us and which today does not exist. [13]

To put so much weight on faith-as-choice asks for a quantum leap from the inherited assumptions of most Church people; at least up to the sixties, one had been used to an almost automatic transmission of Church belonging from parents to children. This could assume the normality of a people's Church with all the attendant strengths and weaknesses. If such a situation allowed for wide areas of religious immaturity, one answer was that Catholicism always sought to be a spiritual home for mediocre and saints alike. The Church tried, in the words of Jean Danielou, not to despise or abandon ...

... the crowd of baptised Christians for whom Christianity is hardly anything more than an external routine ... The Christianity of these Christians can be real, while yet not personal enough to prevail against the current. Such Christians have need of an environment that will help them. [14]

It is clear that Danielou represents a somewhat different response to secularisation than Rahner, in that he would be less optimistic in hoping for a faith of personal conviction as possible for very many people. Out of this sympathy for human unsteadiness comes his less enthusiastic welcome for secularisation. While he will readily admit that 'sociological Christianity' should strive to transform itself into 'personal Christianity' so that 'Christianity as religion' can deepen itself into 'Christianity of revelation', Danielou's comments belong within the framework of the mid-sixties. What this article wants to put forward is a more developed set of 'pillars of faith' for today's secularised situation. The centrality of choice is depicted by its very position in the diagram offered below. But choice is surrounded by four 'pillars' of faith. On its own it might seem to call for an elitist and rarely possible journey of discovery by the individual. Accompanied by the surrounding four other pillars, it is intended to be much less in danger of such elitism. The five put together are meant to be a map of forms of faith that are invited into new life by the very complexity of the secular context (depicted by the outer circle).

How New Contexts Highlight Deep Dimensions of Faith

Pillars of Faith

These five areas of growth are as ancient as faith itself; more particularly they arise in the experience of the early Church and in the pages of the New Testament. Even if called into new prominence by a time of secularisation, they belong to the very nature of faith. Avery Dulles, for instance, has frequently listed three strands in the language of faith as 'conviction, commitment, and trust'.[15] By conviction he means the intellectual component in faith as an assent to truth. By commitment he means the active living out of that faith especially in the struggle of justice. By trust he means the personal surrender to Christ as saviour involved in any prayerful act of faith. These three are parallelled in our diagram by (respectively) *meaning*, *doing*, and *listening*. The fourth here is called *belonging* because it is basic to Christian faith that the Church-as-community is the place where the reality of Jesus can be discovered. In short, the pressures of secularisation bring out some of the old roots of faith into new maturity.

This fivefold thesis can be supported by looking at the pastoral experience of many parts of the world; they represent key sources of vitality in the international Church in recent years. Under the heading of 'belonging', for instance, one thinks of the extraordinary burgeoning of small communities of various kinds but all in search of alternatives to the prevailing anonymity and emptiness of the secular city or to the disappointment of institutional religion as often experienced. A disenchantment with large structures seems deep within the emerging international culture of the last few decades.

Similarly there seems to be a fundamental search for new forms of interiority (what is called 'listening' in the diagram); and this too is in reaction against the vulgar exteriority and sensate life-patterns fostered, for instance, by advertising and popular entertainment. Thirdly, there is a different sense of how truth or meaning are likely to be found today. A theology 'from above' can find itself falling into mere monologue unless complemented by a strong thrust of theology 'from below'. The fourth so-called pillar of faith is entitled 'doing' – from the scriptural phrase of 'doing the truth'. Again, it is one of the renewed notes in the chord that is faith, a note that has sounded itself with more energy in recent decades. In contrast to the European religious scene, often worried about the effects of secularisation on Church life as traditionally understood, one has an excitingly different starting point for dealing with complexity in Latin America and elsewhere. Without 'doing' the other three are doomed to half-life. Belonging can be cosy. Listening can be escapist. Meaning can be merely 'in the head'. Likewise, 'doing' needs its three companions if it is to be saved from the fate of a secular activism unrooted in religious strength.

Tensions in Theology

Our argument, as outlined in the diagram, can be stated quite simply. The forms of faith called for by the pressures of secularisation represent a renewed vitality in fundamental elements of Christian faith. The diagram offers a quick view of growth areas: from their convergence, in many different situations and embodiments, will come the aliveness of faith for the future.

And yet it is not as simple as that. Within each of those four areas lurk serious tensions which, in broad terms, can be described as the tension of 'from above' and 'from below'. To start with the left of the diagram – one of the major sources of pastoral tension today has its roots in different models of Church. The priests of one diocese devoted a full week to reflection together on this issue and came up with the following self-challenge: to communicate Gospel values to today's people means letting go of the images of Church life that have served us well in the past. Where obedience to the Church was a prime value in the past, experience of the Church, for those among whom experience has become a major criterion of worth, is often counterproductive and a source of alienation from faith.

What does one mean by 'belonging'? It used to thrive on a sense of obligation and of reverence for authority. Even if that language still has its place, a bilingualism of approach is now needed. The second language 'from below' will be one that offers a deeper experience of community. The very bigness of the Church can be an obstacle to meeting the new religious needs that arise in a time of secularisation. Through a variety of smaller gatherings of people, a new form of faith is being found in many parts of the world. It is there that a cluster of new hungers can best be met: a need for support, a need for companionship in questioning and searching, a need for sharing and for being challenged, a need for solidarity in some active service of others, a need to voice an intelligent critique of the dehumanising forces around.

Moving on to the 'doing' part of the diagram, one encounters another version of the tension between 'from above' and 'from below'. One simple example of it would lie in the approach to the poor of the world. Traditional generosity took the form of alms, donations, help for those who were deprived. The frightening plight of Ethiopia called forth a marvellous response in this respect when some of the realities of the famine were seen through television. But another language of response is also needed and has made itself heard increasingly in recent years. It speaks of both solidarity and of structures. From missionaries in the third world countries, and from those more fully involved with the deprived, a new form of faith-as-doing is beginning to be known more widely: they remind us of the radicality of the Gospel as a way of life and gradually they are shaping a new conscience for many people. It is as if an underground church is beginning to grow in the new catacombs of establishment religion. It asks for a new reading of reality and in particular for a 'structural' analysis and response to the evils embodied in social systems. This relatively new vocabulary of faith helps also to give relevance to the forms of faith during a period of secularising. As Dermot Lane has argued, twentieth-century rejections of Christianity 'have been aimed at particular forms of praxis, or lack of them, in the face of pressing socio-ethical-political problems, rather than at the particular cognitional claims of faith'.[16] This helps to pinpoint again the crisis provoked by secularisation. It has to do with the relevance or reality of faith rather than its validity as pure truth. It induces not immediately a crisis of belief in God so much as a decline in the plausibility of a familiar church language of piety and passive belonging.

Pastoral Bilingualism

Under the third heading of 'meaning' one can discern another bilingualism of an exciting kind. One theology will stress that the truth is found when humanity stands in a listening position of obedience before the revelation of God. But another tendency starts 'from below' and stresses the long search of humankind for meaning, the role of story, the notion of faith as dark journey of slow discovery. This emphasis is more likely to start its new apologetics from human experience, from the hungers of the heart (as in Augustine), the desire to know (as in Aquinas), or the struggles of conscience (as in Newman).

Even in the spiritual dimension of 'listening' faith, secularisation forces a certain purification of the sense of God, whereby his presence becomes more mysterious in its silent hiddenness and his interventions less easily assumed. In the more personal area of prayer, another shift of attitude may be called forth by a secular culture. One can ask which self is engaged in the strange act called worship? Is it a self that leaves behind something of his or her full humanity at the Church porch, so to speak? What kind of prayer is valid if modernity means 'a movement from fate to choice'?[17] What kind of non-escapist prayer is possible in an environment that ousts the space for contemplation? Like the ancient Israelites looking around at Babylon and wondering 'how to sing to the Lord in a strange land', the modern believer has to discover a maturity of prayer as a counter-cultural act. What is called forth by secularisation here is a new wavelength of spirituality with at least four characteristics that Desmond O'Donnell has spoken of: it will seek a kind of prayer that feeds involvement in the struggles of humanity and that does not get tempted into spiritualised withdrawal from reality; it will be a spirituality that is willing to be on the move and to suffer the new asceticism of God's apparent withdrawal from the world; it will find an authentic balance for today's culture between immanence and transcendence; it will be open to learn human values from outside the boundaries of Church life and hence will reverence truth in all its forms. [18]

It might appear that the thrust of these last few paragraphs has been to dismiss the 'from above' theologies and approaches as irrelevant and to set up the 'from below' as alone of value. Nothing could be more untrue; indeed it would be a collapse of faith into a secularised impoverishment were the essential tensions between the two languages to be forgotten. It is the tension between being 'in' the world but not 'of' it. To start from the secular realities of today is one thing; to stay there is quite another. To start from below means a rich listening to human reality in all its modern complexity. But a human focus will never arrive at the mystical fullness of revelation: without its mystical dimension Christianity is reduced to either a code of religion or a monologue pretending to be a dialogue with God.

In the brave new world of secularisation, Christian faith is called to let go of the note of lament and to discover the more fruitful wavelength of critique: indeed 'faith alone makes possible a critique that is both radical and generous.'[19] More difficult still, it is asked to build up an alternative wisdom from the convergence of its ancient pillars of faith. Pope Paul VI used to say that modern atheism was a way in which the Spirit was speaking to the Churches; this essay has sought to show that the same could be said of secularisation, that it is a situation that invites beyond defensiveness to wise discerning and to various kinds of depth. It also calls for a new quality of dialogue between people of diverging persuasions, a dialogue that can do justice to the unique mixture of secularisation and religiousness that is our contemporary experience.

Notes

1. T.S. Eliot, *On Poetry and Poets*, 1957, p.25.
2. T.S. Eliot, *The Idea of a Christian Society*, 1939, p.59.
3. Alasdair MacIntyre, *After Virtue*, 1981, p.223.
4. Alasdair MacIntyre, *Secularization and Moral Change*, 1967, p.12.
5. Peter Berger, *The Heretical Imperative*, 1980, p.26.
6.Owen Chadwick, *The Secularization of the European Mind in the Nineteenth Century*, 1975, p.17.
7. Bernard Lonergan, 'The Absence of God in Modern Culture', in *The Presence and Absence of God*, ed. C.F. Mooney, 1969, p.176.
8. Antonio Grumelli, 'Secularization: between belief and unbelief', in

The Culture of Unbelief, ed. R. Caporale and A.Grumelli, 1971, pp. 83-84.

9. ibid., pp., 85-86.

10.Langdon Gilkey, *Catholicism Confronts Modernity*, 1975, pp.32-33.

11.Peter Berger, *The Social Reality of Religion*, 1969, p. 145.

12.*The Heretical Imperative*, p. 3.

13.Karl Rahner, *Mission and Grace*, vol 1, 1963, pp.11, 166; *Foundations of Christian Faith*, 1978, p.5.

14.Jean Danielou, *Prayer as a Political Problem*, 1967, pp. 9, 15.

15.Avery Dulles, The Survival of Dogma, 1973, p. 16.

16.Dermot Lane, *Foundations for a Social Theology*, 1984, p.76.

17.*The Heretical Imperative*, p.22

18.Desmond O'Donnell, 'Evangelizing a Secularized World' (three cassette tapes issued by St. Paul's Communication Centre, Sydney). In conversation with the present author he has also brought out a tape on 'Faith for Secular Times' (Veritas, Dublin 1984).

19.Jacques Ellul, *Living Faith: unbelief and doubt in a perilous world*, 1983, p.184

Walking With Unbelievers

It seems right to allow a personal note to hold together the reflections offered in these pages. Although I have been a priest for only thirteen years, it will soon be twenty years since I began teaching literature at university in Dublin. Marxists like to insist that 'context conditions consciousness', and so I would be the first to admit that the university world is not representative and that it can limit one's horizon to one category of people. Nevertheless it presents a keen faith-watcher like myself with some special vantage points. Students are articulate about what their contemporaries may well experience but may lack the opportunity to explore or express. In some ways students can be an advance warning system of the future in any culture: not only are they the most likely leaders of that future, but they are already – or should be – its most alert perceivers.

I now find it wiser to assume that students are unchurched, unless they inform me to the contrary. Perhaps fifteen years ago my assumptions would have been different. Growing up with an exceptionally strong family fidelity to Catholic practices in Ireland, most students would have been believing and practising and largely serene in their adherence. But things have changed. According to the surveys, up to a quarter would now describe themselves as 'ex-Catholics' or decisively alienated from the Church. But many more would be unchurched in a less total fashion: they would practise irregularly or else practise with a sense of disappointment, undernourishment or uneasy half-belonging.

Even already we have stumbled on at least two possible interpretations of 'unchurched'. One can take it to mean a complete loss of contact with any form of Church life. More widely, one can see it as including those infrequent in their practice and even those whose practice is retained only as an outer and inherited custom. In all these cases, Church-belonging seems to have lost its fruitfulness in bringing people to God through Jesus Christ. After all, the Church is only a means to that end. Therefore, no matter what kind of unchurched one has in mind, the aim is never simply to 'get them back to the Church' (as that approach is often understood). As Karl Rahner liked to insist in his later essays, for an older Catholic culture (one that shaped the lives of anyone over forty) the Church itself was the 'invincible motive' and 'obvious way of access to Christian faith'; but this 'faith in the Church' has often retreated to 'a relatively secondary place' in the normal story of faith today. [1]

A Wedding Without a Mass?
It is time to be concrete. From time to time I find myself invited to

perform a wedding ceremony for one of my ex-students, and more often than not at least one of the partners may be'unchurched'. In the case of Susan and Tim (fictitious names, true situation) both of them had been out of contact with any church practice since their late teens and they were now in their mid-twenties. While discussing various aspects of the ceremony, it became clear that neither wished to receive communion; they felt a mixture of unsureness about whether they believed in the eucharist and of unworthiness before a sacrament which they looked upon as too important to be approached dishonestly.

Almost as if talking to myself I happened to remark that it might be much simpler if we had no Mass. Immediately they were interested in this option which they had not known. After some reluctance on my part, this was the form agreed upon, and it proved to be an excellent decision. They felt free of the awkwardness of a ritual that aroused memories of boredom and pain, and more seriously, would leave them feeling hypocritical, kneeling there very shaky in their faith. Once it was decided not to have Mass, they entered into the preparing of the marriage ceremony with much more enthusiasm and indeed reverence. Why, being so long on a road of distance from religion, did they want a Church marriage at all? How could one sacrament seem 'dishonest' and another sacrament 'honest'? Both questions might be answered from King Lear: 'ripeness is all'.

Susan and Tim insisted that they were not seeking a Church wedding to satisfy a merely social convention of the 'done thing' or the 'nicer setting'. They claimed to have a sense of the sacred, to be religious in their own way. They wanted the blessing of God and were more than happy to pray aloud together as part of the ceremony. They were ripe for a marriage (where after all they are the ministers), but almost like catechumens of old, their faith situation did not allow them to be ready for the eucharist. And therein lurks an insight of wider application than Susan and Tim alone: many of those for whom church-religion has faded are far from negative about basic faith in God. Although they may be unsure of Christ and find Church forms unpalatable, they are like those Athenians that St Paul addressed on the Areopagus, when the object of his ministry was to put a face on their known-unknown God. The baptised but unchurched person today is in a similar pre-christian situation – with the complication that their fragility of belief is more connected with Christian rituals, dimly remembered, than with statues on the hill. Pastorally it quite understandable that one sacrament may aid the long religious searchings of their lives more than another. The marriage celebration for Tim and Susan was indeed an occasion of spiritual depth for the couple and for many present. They had chosen the readings with care. They entered into their sacrament as into a garment that fitted them. My homily tried to build from honesty towards hope: their very promises were sacraments of faith and hope and love, inviting us all to be honest about the other faith struggle, the mustard seed that can expand into a sheltering tree. And strange though it seem, the absence of Mass gave me also more freedom to shape a fitting celebration.

The moral of that tale would seem to be that sacraments were made for people, not people for the sacraments. To cite Rahner again, we are still emerging from 'a period of sacramental enthusiasm' which tended to think of grace as conveyed too exclusively through sacramental worship; but 'experience of the Spirit' is wider and more varied than the sacramental life.[2] In dealing with those who have become distanced from conventional Church ways, the faith-helper needs to keep that horizon in mind. His or her primary service will be to offer to people inevitably shy of religious language some chance to voice the important values they try to live by, and to have their goodness recognised (like Nathanael's figtree).

The Emmaus Model

Perhaps the strongest Gospel foundation for slowness in bringing people to the eucharist lies in the great Emmaus story, where the recognition of Christ in the breaking of bread came as the last-minute crown of a journey of slow learners. The two disciples were unbelievers in the sense that they were leaving the community behind. As the final chapter of Luke's gospel makes clear, they were going over everything that had happened in a spirit of sadness. It seemed as if a whole phase of their life had ended in disillusionment and that their hopes lay shattered. Jesus was dead. It was all over – in spite of incredible rumours from some of the women.

The whole episode can be seen as falling into several significant moments. First comes the befriending of these unbelievers by the Risen Lord, in that he walks alongside them, opening a dialogue with them. Next there is his willingness to listen to their version of his own story, to hear out their disappointment ('what things?'). It seems marvellous that the Risen Jesus, he who was at the centre of the story they are telling (even though they do not know it), wants their version of his story. It is as if he has to allow them to express their own experience, even if they have the wrong end of the stick, or even if they were expecting a magic kind of Messiah. Only after they have expressed themselves and been heard, are they ripe to hear the fuller horizon of God. The third act, so to speak, involves opening the Scriptures in a new way, especially in order to glimpse the mystery of suffering in the plan of salvation. Later on they are to remember that their hearts were burning within them as they listen to this unveiling of the ways of God. They were ready for this moment of evangelisation because he had walked with them and listened to them.

Next comes a fascinating little detail: they come to a crossroads and 'he made as if to go' another way, leaving them to go on to the village on their own. It is a gesture of freedom. He gives them the choice to invite him in or not. They are given the chance of not continuing their relationship on the road: it is their invitation ('stay with us') that leads from heart-listening into the sacrament at the table. This five-act drama has an epilogue of being sent back to the nascent Jerusalem church as witnesses of the resurrection.

In short, there emerges a challenging model of faith-counselling from this famous episode, indeed a practical model in six steps:

1. Walk genuinely with those who search, in solidarity and companionship along their road.

2. Listen with reverence to their stories and do not rush in with 'the truth' before having heard them out.

3. Be ready to offer a deeper vision, through scripture, of what they have experienced.

4. Respect their freedom either to go further on the road of faith now or to wait until the time is more ripe.

5. Let the sacraments be the crown of a careful human journey of searching and honesty of dialogue.

6. They can then be fired with a mission to return to others and to share what they have discovered.

Implicit in this whole emphasis is the idea that the relationship is more important than the content of one's communication, and, more negatively, that argument and condescending advice are counter-productive in any contact with unbelievers.

The RCIA as Parallel

Read in this way, that famous Lucan episode can be seen as a precursor of the recently rediscovered stages of the Rite of Christian Initiation of Adults. Its four stages of pre-catechumenate, catechumenate, illumination and mystagogia would seem to have much to suggest for any ministry to those struggling with doubts. Stage one of the RCIA involves a slow listening to the searchings of others – their questions, struggles, angers over religion and yet the hidden treasures of their own life-stories; this healing hearing can lead – often over months – to the threshold of hope which is the typical fruit of this first stage. Stage two begins only when a certain openness has been reached and it moves into an initial catechesis; just as Jesus on the road moved from their pained confusions to the prophets as casting light on their (and his) experience. With many 'half-believers', once they have been welcomed and genuinely heard as in the first stage, this second phase can require a patient clarifying of their often false images of God and of Church. Without getting sidetracked into needless detail or argument, it should focus on the basic realisation that our God is one who has said yes to us in Christ – 'he loved us and sent his Son to free us from our sins' (1 Jn 4:10). If someone distant from Church or faith can even begin to glimpse this personally, they are beginning to arrive at a threshold of new faith.

Perhaps these two stages are all that can realistically be envisaged in most ministry with the unbelievers. It is worth adding that in the RCIA model this journey of exploration would be communitarian rather than one-to-one and it would happily take several months to come to this preliminary decision for faith. In view of my earlier remarks on not rushing into sacraments, it is significant that the two remaining stages involve initiation into the key sacraments and into the life of the Spirit in the Church. Stage three enters into the cost of discipleship and sees baptism as the sharing with Christ in his death and resurrection. Thus it invites the catechumen forward through a careful evangelisation to the threshold of a new love commitment. Similarly it was a long process that led the Emmaus travellers to the table. Stage four fills out the life of the newly baptised (or newly committed even if long baptised): faced with the injustices and idolatries of what is normal for 'the world', it experiences the need to belong to a community of critique and of compassion, rooted in the Spirit and courageous in active service. What is at stake here is nothing less than a new language of self-expression for the Church, one that might slowly rescue us from our complacent conventions and do justice to the hunger of many generous searchers of today.

By outlining the four RCIA stages (in my own words) I have strayed from our central topic. But perhaps the straying is significant. It underlines again the lateness of the sacraments and of a full belonging to the Church in this pastoral theology. To put it negatively, there is a temptation when confronted with the typical unbeliever or half-believer, to opt for short-cuts of sacramentalising at all costs. From my own experience, as well as from the wider wisdom of the RCIA, I fear that if the preparatory efforts of slow listening and suitable evangelising are skimped, the outcome could be a token and short-lived conformism rather than any genuine step to conversion.

To return to our marriage example, I would hope that the preparation and the event itself would indeed prove a step to conversion. At the very least it left the door more open than closed. It healed some of their more immature judgments on the Church of their childhood and adolescence. It introduced them to scripture in a new way. If they still remain unchurched in the areas of clear personal faith in Christ and in being unable to find in Sunday Mass an authentic vehicle of their religiousness, this simply means that they are half way through the Emmaus story as re-written in their lives. Any ministry to the unchurched needs to take the long-term view and hope accordingly.

Three Different Examples

But of course there are other versions of questioning and other variations on ministry in this area. I would like to pause on three different examples of readiness and of response.

Case one: What can one offer when someone like David asks the question, 'What am I to believe?' This broaches a level of inquiry of little interest yet to Susan and Tim. David had not been to communion for nearly ten years but on the occasion of his marriage decided to 'sort himself out' and was happy to invest some time in the business of renewing a dormant childhood faith that he had never denied outright.

Case two: Margaret is a more vehemently anti-Church feminist, whose anger leads her to call herself agnostic. Again the advent of a church wedding to a seriously believing partner makes her willing to re-examine her own religious position.

Case three: James is a generously committed socialist who used to be very religious in adolescence, but his political disenchantment with institutional religion has entailed non-practice for years now and he has real doubts about the kind of God most Church people seem to believe in. Influenced by his more religious girl-friend, he is now asking questions about what faith and Church could mean for someone of his social vision.

Three such varied examples only serve to emphasise the many faces of searchings and the diversity of ministry required. David needs basic evangelisation and is open to it. It is here that I have learned, somewhat to my own surprise, that the evangelists had something to teach me. Faced with a David situation, one needs some plan of response, some programme of points to cover. Culling material from various evangelistic groups, I discovered a set of four steps that can be useful.

A Map of Evangelism

Let me remark in advance that, although the language may be quite different, I think this strategy has something in common with the developmental logic of the Ignatian Exercises (as well as echoing the process of Emmaus and the RCIA). The four steps of some evangelists can be phrased as follows:

1. God has a plan for your happiness;
2. you are cut off from God's plan through sin;
3. you can only return to God by recognising Jesus as your personal saviour;

4. conversion to Jesus will mean living a new life.

No more than the *Spiritual Exercises*, these sentences are not intended to be given to an unbeliever 'neat'; rather they need sensitive translation into the language of each situation and life.

In David's case I spent some time trying to find out which god he believed in (a fairly deist and distant figure) and whether that god seemed to be his enemy or his friend (he was a spy with a telescope). So we had to establish the image of a loving God, starting very much from the hopes of David for happiness in his marriage. Moving on, I avoided the term 'sin' on the grounds that he would be allergic to it; instead we spoke of the areas of life that one would like to have been different and the conversation became a very genuine and honest facing of shadows, hurts, destructiveness, things out of tune. From that it became a natural transition to talk about Jesus and to look at some of the healing and forgiving scenes – the first time David had ever perused the gospel text. And finally, after some prayer, it was only right to look ahead to the values David would hope to opt for in his new married life. This is the summary of a long and enjoyable evening of ministry to David, and for me at least it proved the need for some such plan of faith-counselling. Faced with someone out of contact with the Church, mere jollity and mere exhortation are of little avail: the unchurched need to be taken seriously and when they are open, as in David's case, to some basic evangelisation, the counsellor needs some map of his hopes.

The Fowler Interview

None of this would be of immediate relevance to Margaret. If the various forms of unbelief can be divided psychologically into the thesis of the three A's: alienation, anger and apathy,[3] Margaret would belong within the second family. Her blockages over religion would be much more emotional than intellectual and need to be accepted as such – which is not to dismiss them as irrational or unfounded. Her difficulties will not be met even by the best of arguments; they can only be responded to by creating a contrary experience through some opportunity of being listened to and having a chance to explore the roots of her discontent. Whereas David had finished his schooling at sixteen, Margaret was a highly educated young woman. I found it useful to offer her a 'contract', that is to say, an opportunity to accept or reject a particular form of talking through her situation. I explained to her the outline of James Fowler's 'faith development interview'[4] and after a day or two to think about it, she said that she would welcome it. This meant that we were both going through a structured conversation and the professional nature of it helped to start from a less hostile mood than might otherwise have been the case.

Fowler offers over thirty headings for reflection together but the main headings would include: looking at the turning points of one's life and at the experiences that contribute to one's position now; pausing on some of the important influences, parental and otherwise; how one goes about making the key decisions of life; images of God, sin, death, prayer, change etc. By going through this set of themes slowly, Margaret made some surprising discoveries about her faith-story and about the roots of her anger much further back in a family situation. Even if this use of the Fowler set of questions had not led to such an outcome, it would have been of great help to clear the air. Once again this was an example of ministry to the unchurched that needed certain tools, some flexibility in their handling, and a generous contract of time on both sides.

A More Social Questioner

No such tool would help with James. He is searching for a new experience of Church. It might prove important, as always, to listen to his unique experience and to encourage him to express his conscience over injustice; it would help him to clarify his images of God or to learn about newer liberation approaches in theology, but his deepest need is to discover as alert a social commitment among groups of believers as he finds among his political friends. Where can he experience a living community of Christians? No amount of faith-counselling will meet his hopes and hungers, and the very existence of James challenges the more settled languages of religion in a most healthy way. If many of the usual Church goings-on offer little to attract him (and indeed much to alienate him further), there is a possible answer from the many smaller communities of service and of searching (Young Christian Workers, Focolare, L'Arche, Pax Christi etc.) Trying to meet his needs brings into sharp focus the inadequacy of an older apologetics that placed a high value on the intellectual aspects. Because we have moved from a culture of obedience and of rationality (of a sort) into a culture of experience and of the search for community, merely giving James the social encyclicals to read would not meet his insistence on seeing these ideals in action. I must confess that it is James who leaves me with most unanswered questions about ministry in this area; I am at a loss to see how his needs can be met through any of the ordinary Church structures at the moment. But of two things I am sure: his challenge asks the Church to become what she claims to be, and James is not, in the Lord's words, far from the kingdom.

Which God? Which Self? Which Church?

By way of summary of our three examples, one might say that they each raise important but different questions. With David it was a matter of 'which God?' With Margaret, what had to be faced was 'which self?' In other words, out of what level of herself was her anger coming? And with James the crucial issue concerns 'which Church?' I have found that these represent three of the basic issues in listening to those alienated from the Church. But behind the different angles of questioning, certain traits seem to unite most half-believers. Inevitably they will tend to think of the Church along obediential and legalistic lines: the 'Church' makes the laws (primarily about Sunday practice and sexual morality) and the 'good Catholic' is meant to obey. This stereotype is still amazingly common even in younger age-groups. If they are to have any worthwhile change of attitude in this respect, it is likely to come from having a good experience of a 'church person' (priest, religious, catechist etc.) and hence there is nothing more likely to confirm them in their distanced state than a cold reception or a disapproving tone about their situation. As George Eliot said of the Reverend Casaubon, 'there is hardly any contact more depressing' to a young person than to meet 'a blank absence of interest or sympathy'.[5] The reverse of this comes when the unchurched find themselves welcomed as they are. As in the headline of the Emmaus story, only when the experience is right can the message be received or understood.

Underlying this whole essay is an assumption that needs to be made explicit: there are many ways of belonging to the Church. Just as Jesus stressed mercy and not sacrifices, attitudes rather than rituals, there are more ways of being a Catholic than going to Mass on Sunday. Perhaps we should say that more bluntly to those on the margins of Church belonging – not to diminish the importance of worship, not even to deny the importance of the 'obligation' for those who have faith, but to put first things first. The parable of the last judgment does not quiz people about their non-practice; they are judged on the generosity of their lives. Indeed it is a joyful moment in any ministry to unbelievers to surprise them by praise, by a genuine acknowledgement of the goodness that is within them and in their actions. Such a recognition coming from a church person should never be mere strategy; it is a human truth, spoken in friendship, and yet rooted in the trust that God's Spirit can be alive and active in people who have not yet come to fullness of Christian memory or belonging.[6] Just as in the celebrated episode of St Peter at Joppa (Acts 10) the Spirit today can be at work in many who seem to have lost their bearings in the Church. Not only has the Church something precious to offer to these victims of our cultural crisis; they too can awaken us to the fullness of faith needed today and to the reality that 'the Church is also outside the Church'.[7]

Notes

1 Karl Rahner, *Theological Investigations,* vol xx, 1981, p.19.
2. Op. cit., vol xix, 1984, p. 136.
3. This is dealt with in chapter 5 of my own book *Help my Unbelief,* 1983.
4, The interview format will be found in Appendix A of James Fowler, *Stages of Faith*, 1981, pp. 310-312.
5. George Eliot, *Middlemarch*, ch 20.
6. This distinction between Spirit and Memory is central to John Shea's book, *An Experience Named Spirit*, 1983.
7. Dorothee Sölle, *The Truth is Concrete*, 1969, p. 107.

Imagination and Faith

Jesus Christ never used arguments; he used metaphor.
Jorge Luis Borges

Faith offers a strange kind of truth. It is not like our usual kinds of knowing. For one thing, its object remains invisible and, by normal standards, unprovable. Because of this, sometimes faith is regarded, wrongly, as irrational. But it is always non-rational – in the sense that it goes beyond mere reason.

This essay explores one strand in the strangeness of faith – the role of imagination. But to begin with, we need to recall some of the traditional accounts of how faith differs from other ways of knowing. Aquinas, for example, pinpointed something crucially different about the knowing involved in faith when he saw it as an act of the intellect commanded by the will. More attractive definitions are only translations of that insight into other vocabularies: faith is the knowledge born of love, or an interplay between discernment and commitment.[1] In this tradition of faith-analysis, the claims to truth are met by the role given to the mind, and the claims for freedom are met by the special place reserved for decision. But is this the whole story? Surely a third partner is involved and indeed centrally involved: as well as intellect and will, human imagination is the forgotten vehicle of faith. Theologies of faith too dominated by reason are in constant danger of turning divine mystery into a neat human system. Theologies of faith too dominated by will can fall into two families: either dramatic appeals to dark jumping, or else the severe self-imposed imperatives of voluntarism.

Our more rationalistic theologians will surely object to any elevation of imagination into membership, along with intellect and will, of a new trinity of faith-faculties. Imagination, we shall be warned, is the playground of artists, of people who tell lies that they claim to embody some greater truth. But they are lies, nonetheless, as Plato perceived before he banished the poets. In all this doubting of the imagination, however, what is lacking is a distinction between the imaginary and the imaginative. In some of its exercises, imagination creates the (merely) imaginary, but in other modes it can reveal the (truly) imaginative. Faith is imaginative, not imaginary.

Once again the opposing voices may insist on a subordinate role for imagination. Their strategy is to deny to imagination a full partnership in the knowing that is faith. One can hear the counsel for the prosecution: 'Intellect and will are senior members but imagination can be permitted to hold a respected place as a pastoral associate. Yes, of course, Christ himself spoke to the crowds only in parables (as two of the Synoptics baldly state). Yes, of course our images of God are crucial in any communication of faith. Yes, of course the receptivity of humankind before revelation is powerfully akin to the quality of listening required by great poetry. Yes, of course the whole of the Bible is more literature than dogma in its level of discourse. But let's be serious. Even if imagination has an important role in the genesis of faith, and in the spirituality that feeds the life of faith, it is still excessive to suppose that imagination can be a faculty of religious truth. Imagination – to be generous – often prepares the way of the Lord. But it does not enter into the core of the act of faith.'

In Defence of Imagination

The remaining pages of this essay will resemble a courtroom sequence, where we call witnesses for the defence of imagination against this type of criticism. Drawing on a range of authors, several of whom do not seem to know of the existence of their like-minded colleagues, the aim will be to establish a case for imagination as a crucial vehicle of faith. What will unite these witnesses, is their tendency to downplay the knowledge dimensions, and to stress instead that faith is much more (i) a matter of disposition or attitude that leads to (ii) a special receptivity of searching and listening, which in turn grounds (iii) a struggling way of living rather than a clear way of knowing.

Our first witness, E.H. Johnson, would hold that imagination has to do with 'vividness of mental seeing', and that this is the hinge between the usual kind of knowing and the trust that is so central in faith:

Religious faith is grounded in discernment of spiritual things. It is first knowing, secondly imaging, thirdly trusting ...The recognition that spiritualities are realities can be put into most effective exercise only by aid of imagination ... Faith ... is the work of imagination fortified by experience.[2]

Long before developmental thinking became self-conscious Johnson was speaking of stages of faith, envisaging it as a 'tripod' of recognition, imagining and belonging in confidence to Christ: 'So far as conversion of ideals into energy goes, it is all a matter of imaging Christ.' A final statement from him will serve as a bridge back to an older and more celebrated witness, John Henry Newman: 'It is when imagination sounds the depths of fundamental reality that this reality begins to be felt... that is, to be veritably known and actually faced.' This seems remarkably close in spirit to *A Grammar of Assent*, where one of Newman's constant concerns is our pre-reflective encounter with images of divine reality. He takes the example of a child's imaginative apprehension of God and, while admitting that it is incomplete as theology, he argues that it offers a paradigm of adult faith: it is rooted in 'an image, before it has been reflected on, and before it is recognised by him as a notion'.[3] Many readers will be aware of Newman's distinction between a 'notional assent' (a theological act) and 'real assent' (an act of religion or of devotion); but it is fascinating to learn that, in the drafts, his initial choice of a phrase to express 'real assent' was in fact 'imaginative assent'.[4] His originality in this area lies in his emphasis that faith needs first to become credible to the imagination before it can journey towards a more intellectual theology of faith:

Images, when assented to, have an influence both on the individual and on society, which mere notions cannot exert ...The natural and rightful effect of acts of the imagination upon us ... is not to create assent, but to intensify it ... the heart is commonly reached, not through the reason, but through the imagination.

After listening briefly to Newman, our jury might benefit from hearing from someone who has translated the relevance of these more-than-century-old insights into the more complex horizons of today. John Coulson's book, *Religion and Imagination*, explores the parallels between the experience of faith and the experience of literature, and holds that in both areas it is by means of the imagination that we are 'predisposed to believe'.[5] In his view the 'primary forms of religious belief' are not to be found in formulated truths and creeds but in modes of metaphor, symbol and story. From this point of view, it is a mistake to give precedence to rational explanation over imaginative assent. Coulson would see this as an 'inversion of priorities in religion'. Thus his book begins from the question 'how can I believe what I cannot understand?' and his answer takes the form of a distinction between holding a belief apprehended first by the imagination, and explaining it in more intellectual ways: 'religious belief originates in that activity we call imagination'.

Before calling another witness, it is worth drawing the jury's attention to an almost exact echo of that final claim of Coulson's in another Catholic researcher of the same period. The sociological approach of Andrew Greeley has led him also to:

the position that primordially religion is a function of the creative imagination ...(it) originates in our experiences of hope, experiences which are articulated and resonated in symbols which are stories ... Religious images are a much stronger predictor of world view than is doctrinal orthodoxy. Propositions which exist independent of any grounding in the creative imagination are likely to have little impact on practical responses to suffering and tragedy.[6]

The Nature of Imagination

But what is this 'imagination' of which so many speak? It can seem a slippery term pointing in several directions. For many of the common-sense thinkers of the eighteenth century, imagination was a power of producing mental images of things in their absence [7] and even as such it would be important for any religious perception of a hidden God. But for a later generation, imagination became a god-like and essentially creative agent. So, is imagination a secondary and subordinate stage on the road to real knowledge? Or is it 'the living power and prime agent of all human perception'(Coleridge)?[8] This old debate will find its echoes in more recent discussions concerning the role of imagination in faith.

It is time to call two major authorities to the witness box, in order for both to clarify what is meant by imagination and to advance the claim that it constitutes a central language of faith. The first is Richard Kroner, a philosopher of religion, who devoted much of his life to clarifying the non-cognitive and imagination-centred nature of faith. It was from Kroner that I found my own distinction between the imaginary and the imaginative confirmed: 'The content of the bible is not imaginary but imaginative, whereas the content of poems is not only imaginative but also imaginary or fictious.'[9] Kroner would be openly hostile to any downgrading of imagination as 'the opposite of understanding', and his own works are intended to justify the existence of what he terms 'spiritual imagination', which is central to all religious faith.[10] It is through the medium of imagination that revelation can be received, and hence a theology of faith needs a different starting point than from the one that is usually offered: 'the idea of God must be replaced by the image of God'. Our knowledge of God is 'not theoretical or objective but imaginative knowledge', or at least its

> objectivity must be distinguished from scientific objectivity, because it is inseparably connected with the subjectivity of religious imagination. It is the peculiar and unique nature of ultimate truth to demand the collaboration of reason and imagination; the isolated intellect alone cannot find it. [11]

What then is faith? Does it lose all claims to intelligent truth? Kroner would reply with some qualifications that echo the stances taken by our earlier witnesses. On the one hand, faith is more a matter of attitude than of verifiable knowledge in the usual sense: it is 'the accurate and the adequate attitude of finite man towards the self-revelation of God'. On the other hand, faith should not be too demeaning in abandoning claims to truth: it is not 'a lower degree of knowledge; it is something wider than all knowledge, something different in principle from all knowledge'. [12]

If there is time to call only one other witness to testify at any length, William Lynch will bring our case to a worthy climax. It is a topic that he meditated through a long career, and he can provide some of the most persuasive descriptions of imagination:

The imagination is not an aesthetic faculty. It is not a single or special faculty. It is all the resources of man, all his faculties, his whole history, his whole life, and his whole heritage brought to bear upon the concrete world inside and outside of himself, to form images of the world, and thus to find it, cope with it, shape it, even make it. The task of the imagination is to imagine the real ... The religious imagination ... tries literally to imagine things with God ... The imagination is really the only way we have of handling the world.[13]

From this basis it is a short step to thinking of faith either as 'a way of experiencing and imagining the world' or as a 'world within which we experience or imagine'.[14] In words that seem very close to Newman and Coulson, Lynch would invite us to 'try reversing our images' and to understand faith as 'a first and primitive force in life', something universally operative but pre-rational: 'rationality will later come in' to help in the search for explicit meaning. Faith precedes knowledge but it does need to progress towards knowledge: 'the power and beauty of faith or imagination depend on a progressive relationship with reality, and revelation. Otherwise faith remains a permanent child'. It is no coincidence that both Newman and Lynch take the example of the child to explain the role of imagination in faith and at the same time the need for faith to expand from its seed-bed in imagination. 'Unless one becomes as a little child' can be re-read as pointing to the non-intellectual and non-voluntarist gateway to faith through images and wonderment and listening. Is imagination more than a gateway? Must not the essential moment of the 'child' be transcended as faith progresses into knowledge? Lynch would hold that faith remains stunted unless it finds embodiment both in a vertical belief in God and in the horizontal 'belief men have in each other'. At the same time he would not see this mature faith as abandoning imagination, as a space-craft might jettison its launching rocket. There is a temptation to reduce the role of imagination in this way, by limiting it to an initial rhetoric or affective invitation into the life of faith. This line of thinking would allow to imagination only a preparatory usefulness as a psychological or pastoral tool. In a more recent article, William Lynch protests against this 'belittling' and seeks to establish instead 'the imagination as place of thought', as against a tendency (even among some of our previous witnesses) to polarise the world of images and the world of ideas. Lynch wants us to recognise the imagination as a form of understanding from its beginnings: 'images, and the imagination that creates them, must be seen as bearers of cognition, truth, knowledge'. [15]

If conceptual ideas alone can aspire to valid knowledge, we would seem condemned to a divorced and fruitless language of faith. But when imagination is admitted as a primary colleague of theological thought, then the faith one defends will be one that does more justice to the double mystery of humanity and of divinity. Ultimately it is through imagination that we cope with the difficult docking manoeuvre between a hidden God and a fallen humanity. If that meeting is the foundation of faith, then one touches at once on two reasons why imagination is crucial: we do not see God directly, and often we do not want to hear him or hear of him (the hearing whence faith comes). In this situation of essential struggle, it is imagination that helps us to escape from fantasy and falsehood, to be healed into hope, and to receive new vision from the image of God made man. [16]

Postscript

Our appeal to the jury must rest there, but two further points deserve brief mention. Many important witnesses were unable to be cited this time. The handful that we have heard may represent an intriguing convergence but the club has other potential members. [17]

Finally, one might hint at the possible relevance of this field for a new apologetics. The old apologetics has become not so much untrue as inadequate within a very different cultural context. The new culture, especially in some of its youth forms, often seems a more poetically exploratory one than before. If so, a corner-stone for any new apologetics would be to grasp that the language of knowing God is primarily the language of images. Our colder forms of discourse get the wavelength wrong. A case could be made that the God of the bible seldom either argues or orders; instead he recites poems and tells stories and invites to freedom by way of images. Out of this revelation springs faith, a revelation where imagination is a central strand in the communication of mystery and in its continued life – both as receiving apparatus and as fostering agency. And in so far as faith is much closer to an active attitude than to a piece of knowledge, it will continue to be shaped and nourished less by clear concepts than by the many images, acknowledged or not, that each person has of his or her life and of its hopes.

Notes

1. See Bernard Lonergan, *Method in Theology* (London, 1971), p. 115, and Avery Dulles, 'The meaning of faith considered in relationship to justice', in *The Faith that does Justice*, ed. John Haughey (New York, 1977), p. 13.
2. E.H.Johnson, *The Religious Use of Imagination* (New Yrok, 1901), pp 43, 134. Other quotations are from pp. 9, 187, 63.
3. J.H.Newman, *A Grammar of Assent* (London, 1909), pp.115. Subsequent quotations are from pp. 117, 75, 82, 92.
4. J. Coulson, *Religion and Imagination* (Oxford, 1981), pp. 82-83
5. Ibid., p 55. Further quotations from Coulson come from pp.16, 34, v, 46.
6. Andrew Greeley, *Religion: A Secular Theory* (New York 1982), pp. 48, 68, 98.
7. See James Engell's *The Creative Imagination* (Cambridge, Mass., 1981). See also Ernest Tuverson, *The imagination as a means of grace* (Berkeley, 1960), and Mary Warnock, *Imagination* (London, 1976).
8. S.T.Coleridge, *Biographia literaria*, Chapter 13.
9. Kroner, Richard, *The Religious Function of Imagination* (New Haven, 1941), p. 36.
10. Richard Kroner, *Between Faith and Thought* (New York, 1966), pp 98,101.
11. Richard Kroner, *The Religious Function of Imagination*, pp. 33,63.
12. Richard Kroner, *How do we know God?* (New York, 1943), pp. 98,9.
13. William Lynch, *Christ and Prometheus: a new image of the secular* (Notre Dame, 1970), p. 23.
14. William Lynch, *Images of Faith* (Notre Dame, 1973), p 17. Further quotations come from pp. 36-37, 97, 57.
15. William Lynch, 'The life of faith and imagination', *Thought*, lvii (1982), pp. 14, 9.
16. These phrases draw on some other expressions of William Lynch in his book *Images of Hope* (New York, 1966), p. 209.
17. Other authors that could have been called as witness here include: Ray Hart, *Unfinished Man and the Imagination* (1968); Julian Hartt, *Theological Method and Imagination* (1977); Gordon Kaufman, *The Theological Imagination* (1981); Rosemary Houghton, *The Passionate God* (1981); John Navone and Thomas Cooper, *Tellers of the Word* (1981); David Tracy, *The Analogical Imagination* (1981); Avery Dulles, *Models of Revelation* (1983), and, in somewhat different vein, much of the writing of Hans Urs von Balthasar.

Faith Formation of Youth

The image of objective, disinterested knowledge can lead us astray.
Romano Guardini

In his recent book, *Faith, Culture, and the Worshipping Community* (1989), Michael Warren sees young people today as falling victims to a surrounding culture that invades their imaginations. Hence, in his view, faith formation will require a 'reimagining' of life and of God through experiencing the 'lived life of actual communities'. These pages (originally prepared for an Australian audience) ask similar questions and come to similar conclusions.

In terms of that dominant culture, we seem to have gone through a number of phases or moods in recent decades. Put snappily, we seem to have moved from alienation (in the sixties) through anger (in the early seventies) into a situation of apathy (which dominates the eighties). These are three negative feelings that block the possibility of faith in different ways; perhaps they are a natural pattern in adolescence. But is this the whole story? I think that apathy is often the face of hurt hope, or hidden hunger. My hunch is that what seems like mere indifference can often disguise a real searching and new openness to religious horizons. It seems like the gospel story of Nathaniel rewritten: where he begins from cynical suspicion ('Can anything good come out of Nazareth?), this in fact gives way to the willingness to take up a friend's invitation and to meet this Stranger. Interestingly what happens then is that Nathaniel is surprised by being recognised in his own goodness ('incapable of dishonesty') and once the 'fig-trees' of his existence have been acknowledged (surely something of hidden goodness), he is set free to recognise Jesus with enthusiastic faith. In other words the journey out of apathy comes from an awakening of hope, a positive experience of self, something brought about by 'peer ministry' from his friend Philip.

In my experience, the blockages to faith in young people are less in the order of truth than in the level of self-freedom. They have less to do with doctrinal difficulties than with disappointment with the Church on the level of experience and community. If this is true, then even the most brilliantly conceived and executed programme in religious education will not answer the faith needs of young people now, because what is in trouble is not so much the content of faith as the language of faith within a radically changed cultural situation. What we experienced in Ireland since the early sixties – the set of economic changes that resulted in a much less rural and traditional society – has had its parallels in Australia too. Edmund Campion, in

Rockchoppers spoke of the older and familiar Catholicism as involving a 'people's religion' of 'loyalty to the group'; it is precisely this church-reliant Catholicism that is incapable of surviving in the more complex culture of today. The faith level that would have offered maturity in a more cohesive social context (akin to James Fowler's stage three of faith) will now prove a pastoral immaturity in a situation that calls for a more internalised faith of personal conviction (Fowler's stage four).

In my experience many of the more alert young people themselves are aware of their own needs in faith formation. A few years ago, Irish third-level students gave a weekend to reflecting on how their faith language differed from previous generations and their meeting, of some two hundred and fifty people, came up with the following list of 'faith needs':

1. to be true to its time;
2. to be honest about its struggles;
3. to seek out communities of support and growth;
4. an education that would give them hope for future faith development;
5. ways of praying more deeply;
6. outlets into active social involvement.

What underlies this impressive statement of needs is a cry for a renewed language of faith rather than just an improved programme of insights communicable through the classroom. More precisely, their first struggle of faith is (as mentioned earlier) one of freedom rather than of truth. By this I mean that a pre-evangelisation for today has to face at least four areas of potential unfreedom in a young person's experience. First, there is the Mood War so characteristic of youth, with its danger of being trapped at what Merton would call the 'false self' of negative feelings. Secondly, there are the more social ways in which young consciousness can be kidnapped through superficial values unless they find ways of joining the Resistance. Thirdly, most young people are in danger of thinking of truth in too empiricist a manner and hence need to escape from the wrong question about God. Fourthly, many young 'atheists' are rightly rejecting false gods or inadequate images of God.

What has been compressed into that last paragraph is elaborated in the 'Escape Stories' section of my book, *Free to Believe*. What are the possible applications of this approach within religious education? If our culture causes people to be unfree for faith, then part of the ministry of education should entail both an awareness of these imprisonments and some strategies of liberation on these four levels. Even the inevitably limited ministry of the classroom can offer some nourishment here – while being faithful to its cognitive focus as Graham Rossiter would stress. In the light of the four unfreedoms mentioned, the classroom can provide counter-skills of various kinds. It can present some relevant insights from psychology and spirituality so that a young person recognises the negative feelings which they will inevitably experience (fear, anger, apathy) and through skills of self-awareness learn also to distrust the decisions made from this under-world of themselves. 'Never make a decision when you are down' is a fair translation of Ignatius Loyola on discernment and it is of relevance to the decision of faith.

Similarly, skills can be offered to help people to escape from the three other unfreedoms. Without some education on the 'problems facing commitment in contemporary society' (Rossiter), the emphasis will be too intellectual and too personalist. Religious education needs to be subversive of the secularised 'system' all around; without cultural analysis, for instance of the pressurising techniques of advertising, a faith education will be far too innocent for the 'real world'.

Turning to the need to emerge from the 'fact-worship' of the scientific model of truth, I have a strange suggestion; why not have an explicitly philosophical component as part of the religious programme in senior secondary? First of all, it is in tune with the Catholic tradition of approaching theology only after some philosophy. Secondly, it might well serve as a psychologically helpful moratorium on 'religious' input in mid-teens (when they often say they are fed up with it being shoved at them). But thirdly, an epistemology that would explore thinking tools for the deeper human truths seems desperately needed since the demise of the older apologetics.

What I have in mind here would be a series of variations on Pascal's famous statement that 'the heart has its reasons of which the reason knows nothing'. It would entail some study of the unbalanced emphasis on the left-brain thinking in the last few centuries (scientific revolution, industrial revolution and attendant urbanisation, techno-logical-media revolution and attendant superficialising of the human reality). It is the right-hand brain that is the source of wonder, imagi-nation and of richer interpretations of existence. From this more mysterious dimension of ourselves we confront the great questions, for instance those which Kant claimed were the whole scope of phi-losophy: who am I? what can I know? what must I do? what can I hope for (beyond this world)? Even those questions could offer an agenda for an introductory 'philosophy' for teenagers. They cover the key issues of identity, truth, morality and ultimate meaning. Needless to say they would have to be fleshed out imaginatively in the classroom – perhaps with the aid of film, poetry, story – but it would be foolish to underestimate the capacity of young people to tackle such questions. Because they may not voice them does not mean that they do not struggle with them.

Returning then to our fourth area of unfreedom: many young people need help to name the false gods and so to exorcise them. This topic was eloquently treated in a special pastoral letter from the Irish Catholic Bishops to mark International Year of Youth in 1985:

Some people carry around with them an image of God that is in fact superstitious. It is the image of a punishing puppet-master who has to be humoured and pacified in case he might pull the wrong string ... A surprising number of people look on God as a kind of clock-maker – a God of explanation for the universe but a God irrelevant to ordinary life ... The only God worth believing in is the God who believed enough in people to die for us. The only God worth living for is the One who calls us to live with him, through dark faith in this life, and beyond death in face-to-face fullness. The only God worth searching for is the one who searched for us and who still struggles within us in order that we may become more free to love.

It would be dishonest for education to avoid another and related topic: not only is faith endangered by false images of God but by impoverished experiences of Church. Over ten years ago, a Vatican report on youth singled out the 'credibility of the Church' as a major obstacle to religious faith today. Again and again in meetings with older teenagers and their parents, I have run into the thorny issue of Mass attendance. I find myself coming back to two basic responses. First, it is necessary to recognise that we have shifted from a culture of obedience to a culture of experience; previously, in the upbringing of some of the parents, if authority said something was true or right, reverence for authority swung the issue towards obedience. But in a culture of experience, that same attitude 'doesn't wash'. There is a different starting point for questioning whereby it 'has to make sense to me' or else it does not make sense at all. In this new culture, which in itself is no better nor worse than its alternative, an 'obligation' or 'duty' seems irrelevant unless experience validates it.

My second response to the Mass-going question is an image: if it is experienced as a stagnant lake, the problem lies not in the lake but in the lack of inflow and of outflow. Where Sunday Mass has no living connections with reality, it can only be like a stagnant lake. Exhortations to make connections are futile (I think young people rightly 'turn off' at mere exhortation). Without Sunday supplements, or active expressions of faith elsewhere in the week, the Sunday experience becomes empty ritual, isolated formality, and ultimately unfaithful to the Last Supper. If I am asked what these forms of inflow or outflow might be, I reply with the Acts of the Apostles picture of the early Christians: they had three simple pillars of their faith as lived – prayer, community and service of those in need. Where young people today become active in their Church and alive in their faith, it will nearly always be because they have found some initiation into personal prayer, or some support from an exploring community, or some focus for steady self-giving. Or better still a convergence of all three. Then the Mass becomes what it was meant to be – the crown and celebration of a life lived elsewhere and (as its very name implies) a being-sent into reality to change it with love. One of the exciting aspects of the young Church worldwide in recent years has been the burgeoning of so many small groups that meet these new needs in a rich diversity of ways.

But have we strayed from our topic of religious education? Surely the classroom is not the place for such groups. It is not where groups gather but that does not mean that 'religious education' cannot involve a presentation of what is happening in the different world of 'religious formation'. To look at the pastoral scene today, even as information, is one way of giving young people a sense of the possibilities before them. Possibly the central task of religious education today is to give young people awareness of the ingredients of their future options. If faith is a decision, then they can be alerted to the negative and positive forces which will influence their decision-making. The negatives have been listed here as unfreedoms; part of the task of education is to sow seeds of suspicion about the system enthroned and then to provide tools for escaping the diminishments of our humanity. The positives include an introduction to the growth points of the youth Church internationally, as well as a suitable intellectual grasp of the meaning of the Christian vision. Even though mature faith decision lies more likely in the post-school years, the escape kit can be put together both through the religious classroom and through the entire experience of a Christian school.

In this whole new situation, how can the schools best serve not only the students but the parents? Since there is often a strong desire from parents to have their children in Catholic schools, can not the schools make certain conditions, about parent involvement, parent-education and faith development? If the values of the school are out of harmony with the non-verbals of the home (where religion may come across as marginal or immature or simply unhappy) there will be little hope of the school serving the long-term future faith of the student.

Marcellin Flynn, in *The Effectiveness of Catholic Schools*, has spoken of the possible 'goal displacement' whereby the official hopes of Catholic education are hijacked by other values like competitiveness. More recently Barry Dwyer, in *Catholic Schools at the Crossroads*, has claimed that 'our schools are the most competitive institutions in society'. How then is the school-institution itself to become self-critical of its possibly confusing double messages? The push for success in sport and study can create, within the bounds of the school system itself, an anti-Gospel set of values every bit as dangerous as the oft-recognised consumerism or materialism of Western society. How can this be guarded against other than on speech day and through the impotent mode of verbal exhortation?

Only with reverence for the natural pace of people's searching, can the Gospel be heard with new power, and the only lasting faith for today will be born from a free decision. This in turn makes sense of the sacraments: we have put the cart before the horse in expecting them to nourish faith as if by automatic ritual effect, but when they find their proper place in the faith-journey, they are the celebration of the discovery of Christ and a source of energy that flows back into life and community.

Let me end with two lines from a great Catholic poet from New Zealand. These lines of James Baxter are uprooted from their context to capture something of the hope that I have known to emerge when young people are given a chance to search for an honest faith. Perhaps it is not so much faith that is in crisis as hope – hope that the language of faith can make sense again. Here then is Baxter:

The chorus of their chaos becomes a possible Christ
When the light behind the face begins to shine.

My experience is that what seems like chaos, hurt or disinterest is never the whole story. There is light lurking behind the darkness.

The Tone of Culture:
from Prometheus to Narcissus

In his recent film, entitled in English *Wings of Desire*, the director Wim Wenders portrays two angels visiting the earth. They have the power to observe everything without themselves being seen. For instance, in a highly impressive scene they wander around the huge public library in Berlin, being aware of the hidden longings and agonies of the silent readers, and watching all with a certain detached compassion. The film's early sequences are in black and white, as if to capture something of the desolation of existence as perceived by the visitors from above. Then it changes into colour as they decide to become 'incarnate', and thus even visually the film becomes a celebration of human potentials as against its own earlier evocations of despair.

Sadly, it falls into the old cliché of the romantic ending, with an angel opting to save a woman trapeze artiste from her loneliness. Having so magnificently evoked some of the social and cultural issues of our Western world, the close seemed to retreat to the most banal of Hollywood stereotypes. It promotes the myth of interpersonal intimacy as a seeming solution for all ills and shrinks from initially social horizons to a finally evasive and sentimental image of human reality.

Privatised Images in Literature

One can even find the same temptation and fall as far back as Charles Dickens and in a novel of such social passion as *Bleak House*. Here also the vast panorama of England's unjust systems is expressed only to be abandoned in the end; the novel implies that it is in domestic bliss between a man and woman that the only answer can be found. This privatisation of horizon is a trait of much nineteenth-century fiction. Indeed the whole genre of fiction was born from the needs of the emerging leisured classes. Besides, the very act of reading a novel (as opposed to watching a play in a theatre) is by its nature solitary and private. At the core of the reception of fiction by a reader is a situation that is 'alienated from lived experience', and typically the novel sees any 'key to change as lying in the personal realm of self-understanding'.[1]

These introductory remarks are intended to set a scene for our discussion of the search for happiness today. The purpose in mentioning the world of cinema and literature is twofold. On the one hand, the real crisis of our culture is more one of images than of pure ideas. Hence a question implicit throughout these pages will be how the images of happiness are promoted or controlled in our culture. On the other hand, one of the characteristics of our Western or 'developed' world is that the image of personhood often shrinks into a merely private self in search of interpersonal intimacy as the ultimate ideal of happiness. This again will be a central and more explicit concern of these pages – to describe how this narrowing of human concerns shows itself and to ask about its sources and effects.

Changing Tones of Unbelief

These characteristics in our culture are of crucial influence on the possibility of faith today. Many commentators have identified a certain limbo of lostness as one note in the spiritual chord of the present time. They have discerned a shift in the dominant typology of atheism: it has moved from the more explicit rejections of a 'Promethean' atheism (with its sense of the exaltation of humanity in an adventure of freedom), through a 'Sisyphean' version of unbelief (where humanity is seen as burdened with a struggle that is ultimately doomed to frustration), to an opposite face of atheism that can be associated with Dionysius (in the sense that a cult of spontaneity reigns and old dogmas are regarded as irrelevant and empty). [2]

But to capture the inarticulate and pervasive religious indifference of this late twentieth-century – at least in much of the so-called 'developed' world – we seem to need yet another symbolic figure from Greek mythology, Narcissus. Instead of the active assertiveness of his predecessors, the atheism of Narcissus is marked by self-concern, seeing the world as a reflection of his own self, and by a high degree of unconcern about any more self-transcending questions. It seems strangely suitable that in the Greek legend of Narcissus, the youth was initially suffering from an inability to be responsive to love. As a punishment for this apathy (literally non-feeling), he fell in love with his self-image in a mountain pool, and since this proved an unattainable object of desire, he entered into a frustrated grief due to which, in one version, he committed suicide.

Approaching this theme in other terms, it is possible to claim that our culture of unbelief has moved from one marked by alienation in the sixties, through one marked by anger in the seventies, to one largely of apathy in the eighties. [3] Clearly this is a sweeping generalisation but it has its limited usefulness. Above all it serves to pinpoint some important questions about the search for happiness now: is it the search of an apathetic Narcissus? Is his apathy a sign of his being a victim of his surrounding culture? Might it be the mask that protects his hurt hunger to love and be loved? And how might the Christian vision save the contemporary Narcissus from another kind of suicide?

Individualism as the Liberal Dilemma

In his study and critique of the tradition of liberal thought, Roberto Mangabeira Unger has some valuable insights into the roots of narcissistic individualism over the last few centuries. He argues, for instance, that the 'narcissism' of the self has close links with 'the deification of mankind in the Hegelian-Marxist religion of immanence'.[4] He acknowledges that 'Individualism is so deeply rooted in our thought that it is hard to understand' except by viewing it in the light of some contrary ideal such as collectivism; for the liberal individualist, society itself is artificial and even threatening, 'because all values are individual and subjective'.[5] In the liberal vision of society, individuals are 'radically separate' and there is a 'tendency to abandon the explicitly theological form of the religiosity of transcendence' with the result that a 'secularisation of transcendence' occurs, giving rise to various forms of agnosticism. The best healing of this trend would seem to lie in 'the struggle for sympathy' but typically this natural search for love becomes reduced in the liberal horizon to 'romantic love' with the result that the 'passage from narcissism' is stunted. It is a case of the myth of intimacy ousting any vision of social and faith-based hope, as was mentioned earlier with regard to the Wenders film. Unger sums up his case against the limited images on offer as a human ideal in the liberal tradition: 'every sharing of common purpose appears to be a diminishment of individuality'. [6]

Against this backdrop of the dominant ideology of the 'developed' world – a topic of much greater complexity than can be treated here – one may turn to some present-day versions of narcissism. Gilles Lipovetsky has written a somewhat agonised essay of cultural analysis, lamenting the emptiness of contemporary individualism. He lists its features as 'broadened privatisation, erosion of social identity, political and ideological disaffection, increasing destabilisation of personalities'.[7] He focusses in particular on the collapse of a culture of authority and the emergence of a hedonist 'psychologisation' as a dominant characteristic of the modern self. He links this with many other converging elements in modern society, the cult of the 'cool', the idolatry of emotional self-realisation, the strategies of 'non-stop seduction' in the media and the resultant sense of life as mere 'spectacle'. To cite his own words, 'In a system organised according to the principle of "sweet" isolation, public ideas and values cannot but decline, only the search of the ego and its own interests remains, the ecstasy of "personal" liberation.' [8]

Basing himself on various other studies, Lipovetsky also chooses Narcissus as the symbol of this age, seeing the dominance of this mentality as an all-pervasive technology of control, limiting the human image to the asocial realm. This culture remains blind to what does not belong to the world of intimacy or what cannot be measured by the yardstick of sincerity. Its slogans are of 'participation' and yet its main tone is one of disenchantment. It is obsessed with desires of affective relationships and yet this Narcissus remains a figure of desolation, 'too well programmed in his self-absorption to be touched by the Other'.[9]

Diverging Views on Narcissism

If Lipovetsky represents a rather negative and indeed judgmental approach to the phenomenon of narcissism in contemporary culture, not all commentators take such a severe line. Where Lipovetsky extends his suspicion to the realms of ecology, 'green' consciousness and feminism, other writers hail a certain breakthrough in contemporary times and even welcome the centrality of the self as a potentially healthy version of Narcissus. In this respect, Christopher Lasch provides an interesting example of a writer who has modified his stance somewhat over the years. In his earlier work, *The Culture of Narcissism*, he spoke of North American life in particular as having reduced 'the pursuit of happiness to the dead end of a narcisistic preoccupation with the self'. He saw this as a stage further than the older 'culture of competitive individualism' which had been dominated by 'economic man'; now the stage is occupied by 'psychological man ... haunted not by guilt but by anxiety' and concerned to fulfil needs for 'immediate gratification'.[10] This largely critical portrait of the narcissistic tendency broadened out to consider also the social conditions that produce such a personality: the bureaucratic world fosters dependence; in a social order of large-scale banality, personal relations are made to carry too much weight; the world of entertainment creates a population of fans living with fantasies; in short the 'new narcissist' is the 'final product of bourgeois individualism'. [11]

Significantly Lasch adds some remarks on the religious or a-religious aspects of these develetments: 'The ideology of personal growth, superficially optimistic, radiates a profound despair and resignation. It is the faith of those without faith'.[12] However the same author, in a more recent book, has rejected the automatic identification of 'narcissism' with hedonism, or with 'self-seeking, egoism, indifference'.[13] Instead he sees a 'beleagured' self contracting to its defensive core because of so many threats and radical transitions around. He partially defends the Narcissus situation, seeing it now as an understandable strategy for psychic survival under modern pressures. Thus he is slow to equate it with mere selfishness. Even more emphatically, Lasch thinks it a mistake to use the term *individualism* in a constantly pejorative sense (as Lipovetsky seems to do); instead he thinks of the notion of selfhood as a valuable element in the Judaeo-Christian tradition and as allowing for 'tension, division, conflict'.[14] He would still be a critic of the immaturities of narcissism but he would not want to see this as the only form of modern individualism.

Where this more optimistic analysis is rooted in psychology, another takes its bearings from the world of the new physics. Fritjof Capra offers a still more benign view of the developments in modern culture, seeing new possibilities of emerging from the old mechanistic paradigm of 'competitive struggle' and the arrival of a more 'holistic and ecological view...similar to the views of the mystics'.[15] In parallel fashion it is striking that, at the end of one of his studies in contemporary culture, Theodore Roszac, having defended 'our sovereign right to self-discovery' argues for the need of a 'monastic paradigm' to guide this adventure, so as to integrate the 'need for personal solitude and spiritual growth'.[16] Reading through such authors, one finds oneself confronted with two different judgments about what seems to be the same reality. Is the focus on the self the root of much evil in today's world and in particular of the eclipse of faith in God? Or is it a positive development, a new but authentic note of wonder and autonomy made possible by modern social and economic conditions?

Beyond Analysis to Causes

Such questions cannot be answered without taking other and larger horizons into account. It is one thing to describe these common characteristics of individuals in our culture. But have they a coherent explanation? Just as the Second Vatican Council thought of atheism not as a spontaneous happening but as produced by certain cultural causes,[17] so too the traits of subjectivist narcissism have roots and origins that can be identified. A strong case can be made that this individualism is a predictable by-product of the egoist system enthroned politically and economically in the 'developed' world. If so, the self-concern and psycho-spiritual impotence experienced by many an individual can be viewed as the outcome of the cultural priorities larger than the individual. In line with this way of thinking, liberal capitalism has come to be recognised as a more subtle enemy to faith than the cruder regimes of communism.

Daniel Bell has argued that our typical western systems of capitalism are rooted in what he calls 'cultural contradictions', in the sense that they give allegiance to three contrary principles: a principle of efficiency, or more particularly of functional rationality, seen most clearly in the management of the economy; a principle of equality in the social organisation; and a principle of self-gratification in the culture. The result, as he sees it, is that hedonism 'has become the prevailing value in our society'.[18] Like Lipovetsky and some of the other authors already mentioned, Bell sees symptoms of dehumanisation in this post-industrial society, where 'atomistic individuals' chase psychological 'wants' (rather than basic 'needs') in a 'game between persons'. He wonders about the rescuing role of religion in such a culture, being convinced that the 'real problem of modernity' is a 'spiritual crisis' and that 'some religious answer will surely be forthcoming'.[19]

Idolatrous Systems

Bell's emphasis on going beyond description to an explanation of the narcissistic tendencies as fostered by a specific system, is shared by some more overtly theological commentators. Thus Gerald Arbuckle examines the changing languages of religious life and highlights the 'anti-structure' bias in the cultural revolution of the sixties: 'it was an attempt to make ambiguity and uncertainty, not a mere passing feature of life, but a way of living in itself'.[20] Adapting some of the social research of Mary Douglas, Arbuckle contrasts two cultural models as stressing respectively the role of the group or of the individual. The latter kind (termed 'weak group and weak grid') is considered as 'highly secularised' where even if God 'is acknowledged to exist, he is apt to be reformulated to support individualism and privatisation of religion itself'.[21] In other words, even God can become an unchallenging idol and yet another mirror-image for Narcissus.

A second religious author puts these dangers more trenchantly still: John Francis Kavanaugh holds that in North American society 'our problem is idolatry' and 'its presence is systemic'. In his analysis, the values of the Christian Gospel are avoided in the complacently 'christian' culture that is the American way of life. He speaks of the 'enthronement of the commodity as the center of our lives' and sees this idolatry as entailing a 'systematic rejection of human freedom' in the sense of the potential for 'self-commitment'. In brief, 'we do not walk in freedom, since we are paralysed by what is' and fall into a 'practically lived atheism'.[22]

Still another writer, Michael Warren, exploring the issue from the point of view of youth ministry today, has called for 'refocused attention toward the social forces affecting young people' and he locates part of the trouble in the world of media images where 'young people are continually having their lives imagined for them'.[23] This 'programmed consciousness' involves a trivialisation of human desire and is a crucial way in which a whole new generation can have their attention hijacked into secondaries, so that the agenda of their hopes becomes limited to the personalistic and the immediate.

If our culture causes such a kidnap of basic human freedom, it is possible to go further and to argue that 'most of our difficulties over faith are linked with this lack of freedom' rather than being a problem of pure 'truth on its own'.[24] Prior to any searching for truth is the freedom to be aware of the very possibility of that search. The struggle towards faith today is radically conditioned by culturally induced forms of unfreedom. The typical case is **not** that people opt in selfish fashion to be like Narcissus. It is rather that they are victims of a powerful set of cultural controls that condemn them to this prison of immaturity. Thus the modern enemy to faith is not simply a matter of closed individual consciousness but of socio-cultural systems that, like the birds in the sower parable, can rob individuals of any chance of listening for the Word. To awake to the non-neutral influences of the social contexts is to become aware of the need to perceive Christian faith as necessarily a resistance movement to the dominant ideologies. To think of the struggle in merely personalist terms would therefore be far too innocent for today's situation.

From Judgment to Dialogue

And yet there is a danger in placing so much emphasis on this note of seeing through the idolatries and escaping their alluring influences. The danger is that one can easily dismiss a whole culture in a global way without genuinely discerning it. Too glib a negative judgment about narcissism can result in the religious stance being superior but also insensitive to the potential growth-points for faith within modern culture. Moreover, some note of self-critique is necessary for honest dialogue over faith, and in our contemporary situation it would be dishonest to leave unmentioned the frequent disappointment with the institutions of religion as many people experience them. The Church too is a culture with temptations to limited vision and limited living of its ideals. It too is liable to fall into its own version of narcissism, in the sense of being excessively occupied with its own self. Religion too can have its idols of 'false absolutes' and its several ways of imaging a 'distorted faith'.[25] Therefore, any critique has to include self-critique. It is one thing to discern the confusions of our surrounding culture – its impoverished images, its loss of community, its drifting values. But it is also necessary to discern the warts of Church realities: people are disappointed when they encounter only verbal beliefs, routine practices, or implausible norms.

For a few decades now, Thomas Luckmann has insisted that 'the privatisation of individual existence is linked to the privatisation of religion in general'.[26] In his view, modern industrial society inevitably evolved its own style of 'individual religiosity', rooted in 'self-realisation', in order to cope with a situation where 'subjective structures of meaning are almost completely detached from the functionally rational norms' of the dominant culture.[27] Hence a temptation for religion today is to be content to provide what the spiritual consumer will 'buy' and in this way religion can degenerate into an acculturated product, a source of inner comfort rather than of gospel challenge. To accept this as the only fate for faith would be to betray the communal vision of the New Testament as well as to forget the many cultures of the world where the Western Narcissus holds little or no sway. If it is true that abundance 'increases the power to create isolation',[28] this is far from being the situation for the majority of mankind. Most of the poor of the world cannot afford subjectivity of this kind – a point that came home to the present author when he saw a Woody Allen film during a stay in Latin America.[29] So what we have been exploring here is a significant cultural phenomenon but limited for the most part to the more pampered sections of our planet. Confronting this Narcissus tendency, one seems caught between the Scylla of dismissive judgementalism and the Charybdis of over-optimism about a secular spirituality. Certainly the trap of awareness without action is only a new name for faith without works, but is all the elevation of the self in modern culture necessarily of this gnostic and enclosed mentality?

What seems needed is a reverence for the human situation that allows for a nuanced discernment of the wheat and the weeds within contemporary culture. Of course a key point of that gospel parable was the inseparability of good and evil in this world. Therefore we are always faced with ambiguity. Even in what is called narcissism, seeds of goodness lurk. The hope is to disentangle the strands of 'egoism' and of 'autonomy' within 'Western individualism'.[30] It is a mammoth task.

It seems suitable to end, as we began, with an insight from the world of fiction. Flannery O'Connor, that most theologically literate of writers, once remarked that 'Redemption is meaningless unless there is cause for it in the actual life we live, and for the last few centuries there has been operating in our culture the secular belief that there is no such cause'.[31] In one rich sentence she has pointed to at least three essential conditions for any response to the Narcissus situation. First, there is the seemingly impenetrable shell of indifference. Secondly, there is her emphasis on reaching life as experienced, something that is unreachable by any mere conceptualism or exhortation. Thirdly, by her whole career she sought to respond to this imprisonment of imagination by a strategy of images and parables. Perhaps there are fruitful indicators here for a response to our situation, for even Narcissus-type 'people want to know why they are unhappy in hedonism'.[32]

Notes

1. Lennard Davis, *Resisting Novels: Ideology and Fiction*, London 1987, pp. 12, 121.
2. This three-fold evolution of atheisms is adapted from José Gómez

Caffarena, *Raices culturales de la increencia*, Santander, 1988, pp.21-26.

3. This cycle in a more psychological form is dealt with in two essays here. See pp. 20 – 22 and p. 44.

4. Roberto Mangabeira Unger, *Knowledge and Politics*, New York, 1976, p. 214.

5. Unger, pp. 82-83.

6. Unger, pp. 160-161, 213-219.

7. Gilles Lipovetsky, *L'Ère du Vide: Essais sur l'Individualisme Contemporain*, Paris, 1983, p. 7.

8. Lipovetsky, p. 48.

9. Lipovetsky, p. 87.

10. Christopher Lasch, *The Culture of Narcissism*, (Acabus edition), London, 1980, pp. 21-23.

11. Lasch, ibid., p. 23.

12. Lasch, ibid., p. 103.

13. Christopher Lasch, *The Minimal Self*, London, 1985, p.15.

14. Lasch, ibid., p. 258.

15. Fritjof Capra, *The Turning Point*, London, 1983, pp.12, xvii.

16. Theodore Roszac, *Person/Planet*, London, 1979, pp.3, 288, 290.

17. *Gaudium et Spes*, par. 19.

18. Daniel Bell, *The Cultural Contradictions of Capitalism*, New York, 1976, p. xi.

19. Bell, pp. 22, 28, 148, 169.

20. Gerald A. Arbuckle, *Strategies for Growth in Religious Life*, New York, 1986, p. 6.

21. Arbuckle, p. 220.

22. John Francis Kavanaugh, *Following Christ in a Consumer Society*, New York, 1981, pp. xviii, 28, 44-45, 98.

23. Michael Warren, *Youth, Gospel, Liberation*, San Francisco, 1987, pp. 40-41.

24. I refer here to my own book *Free to Believe: Ten Steps to Faith*, London & Chicago, 1987, p.1.

25. This theme has been well treated in the pastoral letters of the Basque bishops published under the title *Ante el Reto de la Increencia*, San Sebastian, 1988. The references here are to pp. 46-47.

26. Thomas Luckmann, *Life-World and Social Realities*, London 1983, p. 172.

27. Luckmann, *The Invisible Religion*, New York, 1967, pp. 105, 111.

28. Richard Sennett, *The Uses of Disorder*, London, 1977, p. 49.

29. cf. 'Looking North at a World of Self', pp. 131 – 133 here.

30. Alain Finkielkraut, *La Defaite de la Pensée*, Paris, 1987, p. 149.
31. Flannery O'Connor, *Mystery and Manners: Occasional Prose*, London, 1972, p. 33.
32. Ernest Becker, *The Denial of Death*, (Free Press Edition), New York, 1975, p. 268.

PART III: Literature and Religion

Whoever can read the style of a culture
can discover its ultimate concern,
its religious substance.

Paul Tillich, 1959

This section gathers together a number of articles dealing with the spiritual tone of modern literature. In an age when the language of Church has often lost credibility, many people turn to the arts for expressions of depth and mystery. What they find there reveals another and rich dimension of the contemporary struggle for faith.

What has Literature to say to Liturgy?

To pray is to pay attention to something or someone other than oneself.
Whenever a man so concentrates his attention –
on a landscape, a poem, a geometrical problem, an idol, or the True God
– that he completely forgets his own ego and desires, he is praying.
W.H.Auden

It seems appropriate to open these few reflections on the lessons literature can offer to liturgy with a quotation from a poet who was aware
of the contemplative dimension of art. The last few decades have witnessed many efforts to establish links between imaginative literature
and theology, but some of these have seemed misguided: in so far as
they approached literature as principally a source of religious insight,
they neglected the unique power of literature, the fact that its value
lies on the level of experience rather than of message. Similarly, this
essay would propose that liturgy can be inspired by literature more in
terms of a level of communication than in terms of content.

Indeed there may be a particular relevance in this perspective today: the values of literature could highlight a serious impoverishment
of post-Conciliar liturgy in the Catholic Church. One hears on many
sides that the new liturgy, as normally enacted, lacks a sense of mystery, that it has become levelled down to one mode, that it has
become strangely inflexible and unable to answer the pastoral needs
of a pluralist world, that it is often interpreted in an excessively horizontal manner, stressing human togetherness at the expense of
mystical dimensions. In short, thinness and banality have sometimes
resulted where relevance was intended, and a symbolic richness is lost
which has not been compensated for by the easier intelligibility of the
new rites.

Literature, by contrast, has often assumed the functions of worship, or at least of spirituality, for many readers today. Almost exactly
a century ago, Matthew Arnold predicted such a role for imagination:
'More and more, mankind will discover that we have to turn to poetry
to interpret life for us, to console us, to sustain us', and he went on to
claim that 'most of what now passes with us for religion and philosophy' would be replaced by literature. Setting aside the more secular
assumptions of his prophecy, Arnold's words have proved alarmingly
accurate in some respects. In the contemporary culture of the West,
many people approach the value-laden arts of fiction, film and theatre
with something akin to worship and religious hunger. Artists such as
Hermann Hesse, William Faulkner, Patrick White, Solzhenitsyn, Samuel Beckett or Ingmar Bergman have become cult figures in a time of

frustrated religiousness. Where the Church mediations of mystery have failed to speak, the world of story and metaphor has become a substitute scripture and revelation and liturgy.

A paradoxical situation surely. Although the majority of modern authors have been far from any religious orthodoxy, they seem to have formed almost a conspiracy of hidden theology and secret spirituality. What T.S.Eliot (himself a most orthodox Christian) wrote about Hawthorne and Henry James, might be applied to many of their successors in this century – they exemplified 'indifference to religious dogma and at the same time exceptional awareness of spiritual reality'.

In light of this, it could be asked whether liturgy today is not suffering a crisis of spiritual imagination and whether this might not be more central than the more evident crises of creed and culture. If so, the reform of liturgical externals urgently need completion by a renewal of internals also. And it is here that the world of literature could be of special service in reminding us of three areas of possible malnutrition in modern liturgy: (a) the level of spiritual receptivity of a congregation; (b) the medium of symbols and words as revelatory of mystery; (c) the various levels of communication possible within a celebration.

Preparedness for Worship

Both liturgy and literature require a certain level of receptivity if their richness is not to remain unattainable in experience. David Martin has analysed the convergance between aesthetic and religious consciousness in terms of the conditions needed for a genuine 'participative experience'.In this regard some ideas of Karl Rahner on the theme of poetry and imaginative writing seem of relevance here. An essay of 1959 put the emphasis on the 'greatest threat to religion' as lying 'in its human dimension', and on literature as a 'prereligious' liberation of human potentials, capable of 'mediating the indispensable pre-requisites of Christianity'. In the course of Rahner's *Theological Investigations*, at least five individual pieces expand on this basic insight. A 'receptive capacity for the poetic word' is described as 'a presupposition of hearing the word of God', because, in both, man needs openness to mystery and hearing from the heart. But in fact the 'religious element' today is in danger of being out of tune with 'man's genuine experience', when it should be expressing that experience better and more deeply than he is able to himself; and this warning is extended to some overly enthusiastic uses of scripture, as if it communicated automatically to people today. Thus, the preacher of God's word can be helped by being something of a poet, with a poet's gift of telling 'man his ambiguity in such a way that he perceives it'; and this is attained by means of *Urworte*, language that transcends utility and the shallow clarity of appealing to the mind alone. In this respect, creative writers are viewed as capable of saving us from the banal, from being smothered by 'the forces of all that is average'.

Even from this rough summary, it should be evident that these themes in Rahner are relevant to our discussion of liturgy. Does liturgy need to regain the courage to be special and sacred? Has it too easily assumed that involvement means inner participation? (cf. *Sacrosanctum Concilium* 19). More particularly, has it neglected the dimension of interiority in the course of its valid and exciting reforms of rites? These are some of the questions that the literary world would put to liturgy today, in the hope that liturgy would find new means to create wonder and silence, to evoke something of the attentiveness of the aesthetic experience in a context of worship. The success of literature as a kind of private spiritual liturgy for many people today is a reminder of the quality of experience required. Thus the world of literature would join forces with Eastern spirituality in encouraging liturgy to be more slow, silent and solemn. In Hamlet's words, 'the readiness is all'. Preparedness for prayer is our first crisis area raised by thinking about liturgy in the light of the aesthetic-contemplative experience of literature.

The Verbalist versus the Parabolic

In recent years there seems to be a new danger of disobedience to the counsel of Christ that one should not use many words in prayer; and the liturgist does not have to wait for the literary man to point this out: at least two surveys of the state of liturgy diagnosed an 'excessive verbosity' or 'verbal inflation' in contemporary worship. Paradoxically, literature which is rooted in the verbal is also a reminder of the perils of verbalism – of thinking that an accumulation of words means an accumulation of significance. The lesson for liturgy is obvious: if words in drama belong within the eloquence of a human situation, words in worship must be held suspect unless situated in faith and in the actions of a believing community. 'Words alone are certain good' was the chorus of Yeats's first collected poem, but it is a dangerous motto for dramatist or liturgist. It forgets, to cite a rather different line of Eliot's, that 'words after speech reach into the silence'.

And this warning is all the more necessary if the language in question is doctrinal in a conceptual manner; in fact this would constitute a second infidelity to the example of Christ, who never spoke to the crowds except in parable (Mt 13:34; Mk 4:34). Not only from literature but also from the scriptural emphasis on the parabolic, the liturgist can relearn the simple truth that we are story-loving animals and that this has a relevance beyond any mere improvement of communications. If so, our preaching should be more parabolic and less rationalist; it should create echoes rather than offer explanations. Such, at least, would be the advice of Robert Frost, one of the masters of parable and indirection in modern poetry: allow hints to set up reverberations within consciousness, to arouse 'the pleasure of ulteriority'. Or, finally on this point, one may recall a celebrated saying by another American poet, Wallace Stevens: 'poetry must resist the intelligence almost successfully'.

The conclusion emerging here is that liturgy becomes dreary when it limits itself to the language of concepts, when it overloads itself with explanation for the mind, when it forgets the symbol as the most appropriate medium for mystery. The vast success of modern literature as a vehicle of spiritual quest gives testimony to this power of symbol and of story in embodying human complexity and in reaching human hearts.

With regard to flexibility of styles, one of the greatest spiritual poems of this century offers an example: Eliot's *Four Quartets* deliberately exploits high and low styles in contrast with one another, setting passages of rich density side by side with passages of stark colloquialism, thus miming something of the flux of spiritual states. Would it be against the spirit of the new liturgy to encourage a similar and quite marked difference of wavelength between the liturgy of the word and the liturgy of the eucharist? Just as literature communicates at varying levels of intensity, even within one work, so too liturgy may need a conscious variety of levels of action. It needs to be able to range, even within one celebration, from direct human contact through communal inwardness to solemnity. (Another article here describes this variety in practice in a Latin American Mass.)

Four Horizons of Faith

As approached here, literature has been seen as a stimulus for one dimension of liturgy, the sometimes forgotten dimension of depth and the indirect modes of discourse that awaken that depth more truly than the language of the head. But one can suggest that there are four dimensions that enter into maturity of faith, and that if liturgy is to serve maturity of faith, it will need to do justice to all four aspects. The first is the element of the Church as tradition and community of faith. The second is the realm of revelation, of encounter with Christ and personal conversion. The third is the changed lifestyle that results from the surrender of faith, the whole area of social commitment and love. The fourth is the inward or contemplative dimension, the realm of interiority, of one's searching in various ways to find oneself and to be found by God. Post-Conciliar discourse on liturgy has focussed on community, on evangelisation, and on linking worship with engagement in the world – the first three elements. The fourth element of interiority has tended to be not so much forgotten in theory as left impotent in practice. It is the element that literature thrives upon, even to the extent of becoming a gnostic wisdom forgetful of community, revelation and commitment. Modern literature has been intensely religious in its mood and its questions, even when it is largely agnostic in its matter and its answers. Liturgy, by contrast, cannot assume that the religious question is alive or that the religious awareness is alert in a congregation. Hence modes of preparation become vital and a broader ambitiousness on the spiritual level seems essential. Without this dimension, the stress on community becomes cosy, the good news becomes unhearable at any depth, and the urgency of social commitments become unrooted and in dnager of the withering spoken of in the parable of the sower. From listening to literature, liturgy will not solve all its problems, but it will receive a healthy challenge and a reminder that it needs more than intelligibility to do justice to the mystery of God and of humanity.

Yeats, the Mountain and the Temple

Evensong address at Drumcliff church for the opening of the
Yeats International School, August 1982

The time is coming when
neither on the mountain nor in Jerusalem
will you worship the Father. (Jn 4:21)

The poet in whose honour we gather would savour those words in his
own way. Was not a note of urgency one of his great obsessions,
something that stemmed from his foreboding about history and his
sense of tragedy in the age he was given to live? It was a time which
he viewed as deprived of the possibility of worship. Did he not again
and again describe his own spiritual quest in terms, not of irreligious-
ness, but of frustrated religiousness? Rejecting the century of his birth
as a 'century of utilitarianism', he desperately sought ways of worship,
even speaking of his whole work as 'the ritual of a lost faith'.

'Neither on this mountain nor in Jerusalem': the mountain or the
temple. Are not these two wavelengths found within all spiritual
history, two horizons often in tension? With the mountain one asso-
ciates a contemplative, mystical, individual and free-ranging exploration of the realms of the spirit. With the temple one thinks rather of
the more ceremonial and institutional embodiments of religion. Yeats
wanted both, so much so that it became one of his many vacillations
– between the wild and wandering freedom of the mountain, and the
order and liturgy of the temple. Did he not plan a community on
Castle Rock Island in Lough Key for both 'contemplation' and 'mysteries'?

Gathering under his mountain and in his temple seems the right
time and place to ponder those 'antinomies' or conflicts as we experience them now in our different ways. Within each person is a mountain call, to solitude and search, but it seems doomed to incomplete-
ness if it is merely mountain, merely the journey of the self without
forms or guides or the companionship of history. To follow the
mountain route without the temple wisdom is to court what Yeats
would term the 'false mask' of 'dispersal'.

Within each person lies another need for a temple, but a distrust of
temples as we find them. Just as church forms of religion disappointed
Yeats, for us too they can prove eclipses of God rather than gateways
to him. Mere temple without mountain can spell shallowness and
formalism. In this dividedness, as in many other ways, Yeats was a
prophet of our spiritual fate, our unease with mountain alone or temple alone, but our seeming impotence to bridge those two hungers.

In our Western culture now, we are people who know too much; that is our burden. We are kept so busy experiencing and understanding that we can seldom reach more than the threshold of commitment. Like Yeats we remain people of the threshold most of the time. We have respect for mountains, but can we steadily climb? We have reverence for temples, but can we belong and be at home therein?

That Johannine text continues in a different direction, beyond either mountain or temple: 'the time is now when true worshippers will worship the Father in Spirit and in truth'. Truth – is it from me or from beyond me? One phrase echoes often in Yeats as perhaps his most constant question: 'revealed or created'. Is truth created by us or could it be revealed from beyond us? That is indeed the threshold. To hear that anxious question of his could be a step towards crossing the threshold, even if I do no more than recognise that I stand uncertain there, afraid to cross, unable to decide yes or no, cluttered against commitment.

At the least I come to acknowledge my limited but honest truth; at most I could come to glimpse a truth that is not only mine, and a spirit that is not mine. Truth may be in part my doing, but the Spirit is not my doing but rather my receiving, when and if I am ready. And so often our very culture, the culture that brings us to this place, also leaves us unready for the meaning of this place. We come to a place like this to stand at the threshold of some self-understanding of ourselves and of our time. We come to remember a man of mountain and of temple, two essential hungers never in union for him. We come to recognise whether we are ready or unready to go any further than that. We come like the tourist of Philip Larkin's poem *Church-going*, at first dismissive – it is our heritage – and then invited into wonderment.

Is it possible that our familiar tensions of mountain and temple can only be fulfilled in Spirit and in truth? Could it be that the object of mountain and the whole purpose of temple is that encounter with Spirit and truth? One side we know; of the other we remain profoundly unsure, and even afraid of hoping to be more sure. Like Larkin's visitor we look around and may reach, if not yet to prayer, at least a recognition of the wisdom rooted here where our poet lies. In Larkin's closing words:

Since someone will forever be surprising
A hunger in himself to be more serious,
And gravitating with it to this ground,
Which, he once heard, was proper to grow wise in,
If only that so many dead lie round.

A Hopkins Centenary Homily
Delivered at a special Mass in St Francis Xavier Church, Dublin, on 8th June 1989

To this church, one hundred years on, we have come to remember Gerard Manley Hopkins. To this church his parents came for his funeral. They had come from England because their eldest son was dying of typhoid at forty-four. As Anglicans, they had preferred not to attend his ordination in Wales eleven years before, but now at his death-bed in Dublin they shared in the prayers and heard his last surprising words, repeated more than once – 'I am so happy'. It must have been hard for them to believe those words. There was so much about their son that they did not understand – indeed that nobody understood. Of the handful who ever saw his poems during his lifetime, nobody seemed to understand his wrenching of words into unheard-of collusions, into compressions that echoed his own wrenched self. But it is because of those strange shapes of words, never published till he was thirty years dead, that now a full century on, we are here to celebrate his memory, with wonder, with gratitude, and perhaps a tinge of collective Jesuit guilt over how we then left him and his gift unrecognised. As Fr Porter, one of his English superiors, wrote of him before sending him to University College, Dublin, he 'has never succeeded well – his mind runs in eccentric ways'.

To Fr Porter and to any of those who gathered here in Gardiner Street for the funeral in 1889, this centenary celebration would be unthinkable. I wonder if even Hopkins could have imagined this possibility. He so often described himself in the language of failure, as 'Fortune's football' ... 'unheard' ... 'unheeded' ... 'lonely' ... 'to seem a stranger lies my lot'. He wrote of his time in Ireland as 'five wasted years' and he complained again and again of the agony of facing mounds of examination papers, five times a year; they left him 'jaded and harrassed'. In Dublin too he wrote his poems of deep desolation:

O the mind, mind has mountains; cliffs to fall
Frightful, sheer, no-man-fathomed.

But it is also true that there are flashes of self-confidence in his writings, moments when he seems to accept that he is alone on a path of newness and that he relishes it – even if his friends cannot fathom his ways. Less than a year before his death, he wrote to his great friend Robert Bridges: 'The effect of studying masterpieces is to make me admire and do otherwise.'

That doing otherwise was eccentricity for the Fr Porters. For us now, it seems more like the courage of genius. On another occasion he wrote about one of his compositions: 'if the whole world agreed to ... see nothing in it, I should only tell them to take a generation and come to me again'. And is that not exactly what happened? It took a generation for the hidden treasure of his work to be owned by another century, for the mustard seed of his poems to become the tree that we shelter under today.

Those parables of Jesus are about faith and the Kingdom of God. It was the vision that Hopkins tried so hard to serve. Those who gathered here for his funeral knew that. They knew him as a man of kindness and dedication, a man sensitive to the poor, a man of prayer. What they did not know is that he would serve the faith and the kingdom much more powerfully after his death. And to us now the reason is obvious. Quite simply, in our modern culture, faith needs poets and prophets much more than it needs churchy words that fail the drama of the Gospel.

The theologian Karl Rahner once claimed that 'the poetic is a basic need for Christianity': poetry awakens the depths; poetry speaks to the heart of our humanity; poetry forces us to stand honestly at the threshold of mystery. The hard-wrought words of Hopkins have helped thousands and thousands towards that threshold, especially so in an age like ours that finds the usual languages of God unconvincing and distant. Through him believers and unbelievers could share the wonder:

The world is charged with the grandeur of God.
It will flame out, like shining from shook foil.

Through him believers and unbelievers could also acknowledge the numbness that life suffers:

I wake and feel the fell of dark, not day.

But what Hopkins pointed to most of all was Christ, uniting wonder, numbness, everything. He abandoned the trite and tired words of his Victorian time and of conventional piety of any time. He sought words of 'godworthiness' that could do justice to Christ's mystery within all human experience.

That he died with the words 'I am so happy' now seems a summary moment of his vision, his sense of death and resurrection intertwined. That pattern unites his life and his poetry. In his most famous piece, *The Wreck of the Deutschland*, he sought to capture all shipwreck and to search for Christ in all foundering experience. Years later in Dublin he returned to that image - seeing his own life as shipwreck. One windy day, in July 1888, when he had less than a year to live, he saw sunlight coming into the turmoil of a summer storm. And, not for the first or last time, into his struggling self came a sense of unity with Christ Risen, and a sense of himself as no longer a poor joke of a waste-life, but someone precious, like hidden treasure discovered even in shipwreck.

> Across my foundering deck shone
> A beacon, an eternal beam...
> In a flash, at a trumpet crash,
> I am all at once what Christ is, since he was what I am, and
> This Jack, joke, poor potsherd, patch, matchwood, immortal diamond,
> Is immortal diamond.

May his words continue to mirror and awaken both our poverties and our riches. And as he would put it, may he continue to send our roots rain.

Cheer for the Invisible
For the twenty-fifth anniversary of Flannery O'Connor

If Flannery O'Connor were still alive, she would be younger than Doris Lessing or William Golding. Her death, on 3rd August 1964, several months short of her fortieth birthday, was an enormous loss to literature in general and to Catholic writing in particular. At the age of twenty five she learned that she had lupus, the incapacitating disease that had killed her father, but in the fourteen years that remained to her, she managed with increasing difficulty to produce practically all her major writings. Behind her she left two novels (*Wise Blood* and *The Violent Bear it Away*), a few dozen short stories, a collection of essays (*Mystery and Manners*) and a unique and large set of letters which appeared as *The Habit of Being*.

In the quarter of a century since her death she has been the subject (or object) of considerable critical commentary. At least twenty books have been published on her work and many more doctoral dissertations produced about her. Since 1972 a journal entitled *The Flannery O'Connor Bulletin* has appeared annually. She herself would cast a cold eye on this Interpretation Industry in so far as it believed that 'you read the story and then climb out of it into the meaning'. For her the interaction of story and meaning was much more subtle and rooted in her self-taught but traditional theology.

Apart from reading Aquinas for twenty minutes every night, this lay-woman from rural Georgia studied (and often reviewed) some of the major religious thinkers of mid-century: Maritain, Mounier, Rahner, de Lubac, Teilhard, Barth, Guardini. With some justice she described herself as 'no vague believer' but someone for whom 'the meaning of life is centered in our Redemption by Christ'. Since she was acutely aware of how 'redemption is meaningless' within modern culture, her stories became her strategy of non-didactic assault on the securities of the secular imagination. 'My audience', she wrote, 'are the people who think God is dead'; 'my subject in fiction is the action of grace in territory held largely by the devil'. Reviewing Vawter's *The Conscience of Israel*, she described the mission of the prophet 'to recall the people to truths they were already aware of but chose to ignore'. In something of this light she saw her own vocation as a novelist.

Thus she was probably the most theologically equipped of fiction writers in England since George Eliot. What she remains famous for are stories that seem like grotesque thrillers and yet conceal an element of comic-cum-religious shock. Although the outer setting of many of her tales is the Bible Belt South, the sense of grace is profoundly Catholic. One of her letters of 1955 portrayed herself as 'a

Catholic peculiarly possessed of the modern consciousness, that thing Jung described as unhistorical, solitary, and guilty. To possess this within the Church is to bear a burden, the necessary burden for the conscious Catholic'. Apart from her deep Catholic commitment, at once spiritual and intellectual, the other influence that she embraced was her Southern origin. In her view to live in the 'Christ-haunted South' was to be 'doubly blessed, not only in our Fall, but in having means to interpret it'. Frequently she adopted a sarcastic tone about the superficialities of the Yankee North. When someone lamented the alienation of the South, she replied that it was not alienated enough. In similar vein, and towards the end of her own life, she commented that the funeral of President Kennedy 'was a salutary tonic for this back-slapping gum-chewing hiya-kid nation'.

All this could seem dour. Flannery O'Connor was a serious woman, a proud southerner, a demanding Catholic, a sharp critic of nonsense; but she was a joyous comedian as well, someone for whom 'happiness' was bigger than 'non-misery'. Asked by one interviewer about the effect of her paralysis on her work, she retorted characteristically that for writing she used her head, not her feet. It was typical of her to write of herself on crutches as 'a structure with flying butresses'. The Irish novelist Brian Moore once remarked that he had found her stories a little off-putting in their strangeness until he read the volume of her letters and realised that spirit of wit that possessed her. When Cardinal Spellman produced a large novel called *The Foundling* and devoted the profits to an orphanage, she was unsparing in her discernment: buying the novel might help the orphans but not the quality of Catholic literature, but 'you can always use the book as a doorstop'. She is dismissive of many superficialities, from pious Catholic approaches to literature to the equally sentimental secularist who 'wants either his senses tormented or his spirits raised by fiction: his sense of evil is diluted or lacking altogether, and he has forgotten the price of restoration'.

Hence the wit of her fiction was aimed at the defence mechanisms of atheistic pride in the modern world – at least indirectly. Through moments of comic surprise she seeks to expose both character and reader to a conversion of consciousness from rigidity to reverence. This is the drama of grace. In one of her letters she wonders 'if anybody can be converted without seeing themselves in a kind of blasting annihilating light, a blast that will last a lifetime'. That sentence now seems marvellously revealing for her own purposes as a writer. Her stories aim to blast open the complacencies. In one of them, *Good Country People*, a nihilist woman philosopher has her wooden leg robbed by a travelling Bible salesman whom she tried to seduce!

The plot is deliberately grotesque (one of her favourite words) but its rhythm of details remains at once realist and hauntingly analogical (a term she would prefer to symbolic). Through a total fidelity to the visible, and a comedy of human angularity, she leads the reader to a confrontation with the invisible, with grace and mystery.

In the last winter of her life she completed one of the most compassionate yet comic of her religious stories. *Revelation* traces the awakening of Mrs Turpin to her own fragile status as a Christian and ultimately to the differentness of God. Located as always in utterly credible settings – a doctor's waiting room and later a pig farm – her smugness undergoes a kind of shock therapy. At one moment in the waiting room (and one brilliantly prepared in the narrative), Mrs Turpin is crowing out her thanks to Jesus 'for making everything the way it is', only to have a scowling girl fling a book (called *Human Development*) at her eye and call her a 'wart hog' from hell. This first dent to her armour fuels a rage against God and she finds herself roaring at him across the pigs, 'Who do you think you are?' But her question returns as an echo 'like an answer', and the story ends with her vision of a procession of hordes of people she had despised 'rumbling toward heaven', while her own type of respectable believers bring up the end of the procession with 'even their virtues' being burned away. These few lines of paraphrase are an injustice to the dense yet lucid drama of the text but they may serve to stimulate readers to seek the original. In *Revelation*, as in so many others, they will discover one of the most challenging story-tellers of modern times, someone whom Thomas Merton insisted on comparing more with Sophocles than with Hemingway.

One may end with a flash of her own humour and wisdom. Flannery O'Connor had the hobby of keeping peacocks and used to love watching people's reaction to the spectacle of them spreading their magnificent tails. Most of their remarks, she noted, 'show the inadequacy of human speech ... the usual reaction is silence, at least for a time'. She never encountered laughter at this moment. Then she recounts how the peacock often combines the lifting of the tail with the raising of his voice:

He appears to receive through his feet some
shock from the centre of the earth, which
travels upward through him and is released:
Eee-ooo-ii! Eee-ooo-ii! To the melancholy
this sound is melancholy and to the hysterical it
is hysterical. To me it has always sounded
like a cheer for an invisible parade.

Her own voice is still cheering for the invisible.

Beckett: the Honesty of Absence

*She tried to fancy what the flame of a candle looks like
after the candle is blown out.*
Lewis Carroll

That he was born on Good Friday and died at Christmas seems only
right for someone who reversed so many expectations. When he was
awarded the Nobel Prize, the citation – in another paradox – praised
the richness with which he explored essential human poverty. His
genius was to be able both to celebrate and chide our hungers. One
of his favourite jokes was overheard (surely in Dublin) on a building
site, when one worker called to another, 'Don't come down the
ladder, I've taken it away.' With the ladder of meaning absent, his
pendulum swung, as he remarked of Proust, between Suffering and
Boredom. And yet the compulsion of language tempts us to think
there must somehow be meaning, or at least to keep blathering to
cover its absence.

As against Joyce, whom he saw as seeking 'omnipotence as an
artist', Beckett chose to work with 'impotence, ignorance' adding
that 'anyone nowadays who pays the slightest attention to his own
experience finds it the experience of a non-knower, a non-can-er'.
In this way his art was 'the apotheosis of solitude; there is no communication because there are no vehicles of communication'. Some
might see that litany of grim terms – suffering, boredom, impotence,
solitude, absence – as an adequate summary of his work. They would
view him as a master of pessimism, even of nihilism and despair. But
to judge only the paraphrasable content is a travesty of his writings as
art. It was the mistake of Plato over the poets and it remains a frequent pitfall for religious believers confronted with the seemingly
radical atheism of modern literature. Can the process and experience
of art be reduced to an *ism*? Will not any worthwhile piece of theatre
or fiction frustrate our longings for neat clarities and concepts and
instead hit us below the belt of reason? And was not Beckett a rebel,
at once lucid and complex, against any easy 'messages'? For him
performance was all.

In this light one can look again at his most celebrated play. *Waiting
for Godot* begins with a silent mime before its first word is spoken.
The mime is of failure (twice), the word is 'nothing', and the situation
is one of basic comedy – a man trying to take off his boot and not
being able to. To concentrate on the 'theme' of impotence, or to
stress the bleakness of 'nothing to be done', without experiencing the
music-hall playfulness of that physical opening, could intellectualise

the scene out of its only genuine space of existence, which is in a theatre and before an audience.

A more subtle danger is risked by Christian commentators on the play. When it first appeared, *The Times Literary Supplement* voiced the opinion that it was a 'modern morality play, on permanent Christian themes'. The evidence for such a conclusion is substantial but the conclusion still sounds naïve. Some have taken it as a Passion story, with the tree, the one object on the barren stage, as a traditional symbol of the Cross. They point to the almost death and resurrection of Lucky, the suffering servant, who is practically killed by the others for speaking the prophetic truth about humanity, and then raised up. Then there is new life from the tree in Act II: it springs leaves overnight. Others have seen the play as playing with the tensions between incarnational and transcendent theologies. Perhaps Godot does come in the shape of Pozzo and Lucky but the two waiting tramps are expecting a Godot from beyond, and so cannot recognise the Godot who comes. In this respect it is fascinating to note a change of stage directions that Beckett made in later editions. When Pozzo and Lucky depart for the second time, Estragon wonders aloud to Vladimir, 'Are you sure it wasn't him?' and the reply is a triple 'Not at all!' In the early versions the text put in a simple instruction to 'pause' between the second and third rejection of Estragon's hunch. But later the actor is given more explicit instructions ('less sure', 'still less sure') which seem to open further the possibility of a Godot having come unrecognised. And yet all these Christian hints and images are only part of the echo chamber of the play; they tease as metaphors but provide no foothold for meaning.

In a slightly different way, one can argue that the play presents a composite picture of humanity, rather than four or five individuals. Two stand still, waiting, talking, wondering, a summary of inner life, with its alienation and isolation. Two keep on the move, progressing but declining, a summary of history, with its cries and cruelties. Of the two who wait, one is more speculative, the man with the hat and the inventive metaphors; the other is more earthy, the man with the boots and the nightmares. Of the two who travel, one is master and the other is slave. Lucky's only speech is a famous piece of chaos that mocks and dismantles the pretensions of 'progress'. Although it seems incoherent, a core of simple lament survives through the parody. Surrounded by ridiculous lists of the achievements of academia or science or sport, it presumes the existence of a personal God 'with white beard quaquaquaqua outside time' but insists that 'man ... in spite of the progress ... wastes and pines'. If *quaquaquaqua* seems a playful send-up of pompous God-talk, still Beckett's work is seldom silent on the possibility of God. His play is not a version of athe*ism* but a theatrical evocation of metaphysical absence set over against the other ordinary absence, the simple fact of human unfulfilment.

Does not the very title of the play contain the word 'God', at least as a trace or an echo? Could not the 'ot', as pronounced in French, be a rising cry of pain as over loss or absence? At least the play seems the 'tragicomedy' (Beckett's carefully chosen word on the title page) of the human inability to accept meaninglessness. In Beckett's world, we seem to have an unquenchable, if unanswerable, hope for some saving presence. As a result, we are comically and tragically incapable of conclusive despair.

But to discuss Godot in this way could ignore or forget the feel of the play in performance; it is there, and there only, that Beckett should be judged. In one of his rare cooperative moments with interviewers, Beckett once related *Waiting for Godot* to a sentence in St Augustine: do not despair, one of the thieves was saved; do not presume, one of the thieves was damned. But he was leading his listener up a logocentric path, dangling a bait of easy thematic explanation before him. So it is all about salvation and damnation ... Mischievously he added that the sentence, especially in Latin, has a wonderful shape and 'it is the shape that matters'. All our tempting theologisings about him deserve a similar rebuke. They have a certain interest but the work transcends the urge to kidnap or pin down, or interrogate it from a fixed stance.

Towards the end of his recent book, *Real Presences*, George Steiner comments that 'where God's presence is no longer a tenable supposition and where His absence is no longer a felt, indeed overwhelming weight, certain dimensions of thought and creativity are no longer attainable'. Samuel Beckett never escaped that burdened sense of God's absence. Indeed he was closer, in his own tongue-in-cheek way, to the long tradition of negative theology, of which Henri de Lubac once wrote, 'although it is negative and remains negative, it is the very opposite of negation'.

The Gnostic Lure of Literature

The spirituality of this unchurched era may be found in products of the literary imagination rather than in more orthodox locations. For better or worse, this seems to be a cultural fact, at least for many in our Western society. To root this claim in one example, I ask myself what work of theology or spirituality has had the same impact on me as Ermanno Olmi's film *The Tree of the Wooden Clogs*? Its uniqueness lay in its courage to evoke the dimension of mystery through the ordinary; in this sense, and without hardly a word of 'message', it managed to awaken a dormant sense of worship in many of its secular viewers.

To argue in this manner, that the imagination can be the privileged vehicle of religious awareness, is not an original thesis. Even for those confused by creeds or bemused by churches, religious feeling has seldom vanished or died. Very few actually close the book on God and hardly anyone claims to live with atheist security. So it is to this limbo of frustrated religiousness that the value-laden arts speak now with special power. Today literature and film and drama are both gifted and burdened with a historically new role of preserving religious wonderment in this dark age of conceptual and social confusion.

Versions of this argument are legion: we have seen a plethora of footnotes to Shelley's claim that poets are the unacknowledged legislators of the world, or to Arnold's amendment of it to read that poetry would soon replace religion. But concerning such sweeping immanentism there are many questions to be asked, and, in this respect, T.S.Eliot pronounced judgment on some of his fellow writers and their readers:

> The number of people in possession of any criteria for discriminating between good and evil is very small; the number of the half-alive hungry for any form of spiritual experience, or what offers itself as spiritual experience, high or low, good or bad, is considerable. My own generation has not served them very well.

In his view, Yeats's 'supernatural world' had little 'spiritual significance', just as Lawrence's vision was 'spiritual but spiritually sick'. [1]

One does not have to follow this somewhat testy Eliot (from a book he never allowed to be reprinted) in order to be impressed by the questions raised. If modern literature provides a spirituality for today, is this automatically a healthy phenomenon? Is any spirituality better than none? Or could it be that the cult of modern literature, far from being a form of pre-evangelisation, could lure the elite into a new gnosticism, offering all the attractions of spiritual exploration without any of the challenges of religious commitment? Once again, one can cite a classic confrontation of attitudes between Eliot and Yeats. Eliot objected to the title of Yeats's last play: 'I cannot accept a Purgatory in which there is no hint, or at least no emphasis upon purgation.' Yeats, by contrast, criticised Eliot's 'tendency to exchange search for submission'.[2] That last phrase neatly captures the terms of our debate, in that one kind of imagination thinks of itself as embodying our perpetual quest for making sense through images; but could it be that the powerful variety with which imagination pursues this 'search' may make 'submission' to any faith seem impossible, unreal, and even a little vulgar?

The problem can be pinpointed further through some words of Karl Rahner, talking not specifically of literature, but of what he calls 'the basic difficulty for all of us today':

All of us, even the atheist who is troubled and terrified by the agonising nothingness of his existence, seem to be able to be religious in the sense that we reverence the ineffable in silence, knowing that there is such a thing. It strikes us only too easily as an irreligious indiscretion, almost as bad taste vis-à-vis this silent and religious reverence before the absolute mystery, when we not only talk about the ineffable, but when beyond that we point our finger as it were at this or that particular thing among the usual pieties within the world of our experience and say: there is God. [3]

This rings true as a summary of what one might call the threshold stance in modern imagination, open towards some kind of religiousness, but unconvinced by any religious mediations. Our question becomes whether this clinging to a threshold posture may be a necessary heresy of the modern imagination. Hegel speaks somewhere of adoration of the question mark, and certainly this level of interrogative energy seems to have characterised the classic writers of modernism. If they have a doctrine, it is, as Lionel Trilling liked to lament, one of subversive negation of the anchors of ordinary life.

From late Hardy or late James through Conrad to Lawrence, the great tradition has been one of metaphysical satire, often stronger in its underminings than in its tentative affirmations. Thus Lawrence can be embarrassingly preachy when trying to praise or to celebrate, and then frighteningly memorable in his dramatising of the half-lives of industrial high society.

The phenomenon of modernism in literature – a movement now some seventy years ago – aroused suspicions of 'heresy' in the mind of Eliot, but he did not name it. Others have done so and indeed it is not unusual to find the term 'gnostic' applied to a whole cluster of tendencies in modern culture. Thus Jung wrote, in the early thirties, that the 'spiritual currents of the present' have 'a deep affinity with

Gnosticism', in that people sought to explore their inner selves 'without reference to any traditional creed', stressing 'knowledge instead of the faith which is the essence of Western religions.' [4]

In Jung, as in many others, the extension of the term from the world of ancient religion is seen as characterising more a mood of modern searching than any clear contents or doctrines. And, as Eric Voegelin has frequently stressed, contemporary gnosticism offers itself as 'ersatz religion', marked by a throwback into the world of myth, a radical 'receding from transcendence' into that 'immanentisation' and 'self-salvation' found in Marx, Nietzsche, Heidegger, Nazi politics and, more recently, structuralism; in his words, 'modernity is defined as the growth of gnosticism'. In this way, one finds the 'derailment' of man into a 'magic dream', where 'faith and the life of the spirit are expressly excluded as an independent source of order in the soul'.[5]

An example may keep our feet on the ground. Why did Hermann Hesse become a best-seller again in the early seventies? The League for Spiritual Discovery found in him a kindred spirit, an answer to their need for 'mystics without mysticism', as Hugo von Hofmannsthall had long previously termed it. Indeed Hesse himself acknowledged his gnostic leanings, in that his theology was more like a spiritual psychology, and his faith was grounded in aesthetics. In his novels, one can trace the typically gnostic moods of modern literature in their most overt and eloquent form: there is the preference for a-historical intuitions and for a symbolic language of alienation.

A central character in Hesse will awaken from drift into guilt; he will explore the dualistic drama of his own self, with a sense of dark fatedness and disorder rather than any sense of responsible sin. He will journey through outer and inner adventures until he emerges into some moment of magical unity, and this experience will present itself as salvific in terms of intensity and awareness. The focus will stay at this level of immanent mysteriousness rather than involve any passover to transcendent Mystery. In this way Hesse is a perfect exemplar of the threshold stance and of the gnostic arrival at a primal innocence, and it is not surprising to find him described as 'the most unequivocal manifestation of Romantic Gnosticism in the twentieth century'. [6]

It is easy enough to single out other cases of gnostic content in modern literature. An obvious one would be Yeats (again), who described himself in his *Autobiography* as being 'very religious', yet deprived of the 'religion of my childhood' and forced therefore to construct a 'new religion, almost an infallible church of poetic tradition'.[7] But the title of this article is not 'the lure of gnostic literature'; it is phrased otherwise to suggest that the crux lies more in the context than in the content. The focus of our question is not so much the existential content of great visionaries of imagination in this century as the reception of their vision by the average reader of such literature. The gnostic problem, if such there be, lies less in the vision alone than in the receiver and in his horizon.

I am not for a moment saying that it is the job of literature to lead readers across the threshold into some religious commitment. The glory of literature is to be language 'on holiday' (Wittgenstein's phrase) and hence free of the burden of any merely didactic rhetoric. But a spiritual problem arises with readers who are so taken by a world of vague symbols that they can give no credence to any other form of truth. If this happens, then the latent gnosticism of modernist imagination becomes a lived gnosticism, an inability to trust any horizons of truth beyond the fictive. So the spiritual potential of literature becomes a narrowing immanentism by reason of the perspective of its readers rather than by any inherent failure of writer or medium.

To return to that dangerous word 'heresy': I am arguing that the gnostic heresy today is found less in the great works of imagination than in the environment that inflates their wisdom into the only possible mode available. Indeed it can be a working definition of heresy to say that it is not so much a falsehood as a truth without a context that therefore becomes falsified. Literature, by its very specialisation as a mode of meaning, tends to occupy a zone of unreason and of indirection, but it may well find this inescapable gnosticism magnified because of the absence today of other forms of credible wisdom. It is the isolation of imagination that leads to the lure of gnosticism.

Jean Guitton has shown that every great heresy is rooted in 'the structure and the depth of the human mind', and so, far from being a transitory phenomenon in one moment of theological history, heresies are recurrent and permanent attractions of mankind under pressure. Indeed Guitton has stressed gnosticism as 'the most profound' of 'all the temptations of the mind', as one of the 'great partial choices that mark the history of man'. It is rooted in dissociation and in a denial of history and of time: out of a sense of crisis, the mind panics and opts for images of light. In Guitton's words, 'modern man is caught between the mysterious depth of God, and the absurd depth of his own being. Faith gives us the first, gnosticism the second'.[8] And of the second modern literature has furnished the most compelling images.

Some of these images – as in Hesse or more subtly in Patrick White – belong to the finest spiritual rhetoric of this century. In this sense White has spoken of his corpus of fiction as intended 'to give professed unbelievers glimpses of their own unprofessed factor ... a religious factor'.[9] Certainly the cycle of his seven novels, from *The Tree of Man* in 1956 to *A Fringe of Leaves* in 1976, can now be seen as constituting the most impressive theodicy in fiction since Dostoevsky. It remains, however, a highly heterodox theodicy, angular and eccentric not only in its spiritual quest but in its glimpses of God.

There are other purveyors of gnosticism who merit less respect: one might single out Peter Shaffer's *Equus* as a classically decadent success of recent theatre. Although he uses some avant-garde stage techniques with finesse, 'significant issues' are raised only as a form of 'intellectual titillation'.[10] *Equus* should have been called 'Horse': its title is only the first of its gnostic obfuscations. It pretends to be concerned with a major theme – the shrinking of existence when it involves no worship, no passion, no mystery. But its treatment remains merely glib, a version of Nietzsche made nice, and the vast popularity of such a play seems to indicate audiences who prefer mystification to mystery. Thus *Equus* is an example not only of gnostic fuzziness of content but of a gnostic culture easily deceived into taking voyeuristic cleverness to be spiritual depth. It is an old temptation and a familiar fall, reminiscent of Eliot's words (cited earlier) on half-alive hunger, or of Allen Tate's celebrated discussion of the 'angelic imagination' where feeling becomes 'occulted' and where people try to circumvent the incarnate world in their reaching 'for transcendental meanings'. [11]

Once one begins to identify the whiff of gnosticism in modern culture, rather like coming to know the odour of hash, it can be detected with surprising frequency. If heresy, as was being proposed earlier, is a lonely form of truth, one that has lost its companion forms of wisdom, then the prevalence of gnosticism is only a sympton of cultural trouble. If it is the nature of every deep heresy to exaggerate a deep truth, modern gnosticism is no exception, nor is it at all surprising that it should infiltrate the world of literature today. It stems from the fact that conceptual clarities and institutional structures of meaning usually leaves our hungers unsatisfied. It stems from the unprecedented collapse of older cultural props in the last two or three generations. In such a context it seems safer to embody truth in stories that to affirm it in concepts or to live it in commitments. And so the symbolic mode, with its power and its limitation, moves to the centre of the epistemological stage in the lives of many people. When Churches fail to convince and when Revelation seems unreal, poetry, drama, fiction and film assume new roles as mediators of ultimate questioning.

The deep truth here is that imagination can do more justice to mystery than other forms of discourse. The heart finds more ravishment and more fullness along the road of symbols than in any other language save love. The shadow truth appears when imagination becomes not a transparency but a terminus, when the truths of symbols lose their contact with other truths. At this point exclusivity becomes distortion and one finds the sure signal of the heretical – *sola scriptura, sola ecclesia, sola actio, sola imaginatio.* That four-letter word is always there when we lose touch with the variety of forms of wisdom and grope for an extreme but isolated solution.

Our debate here on the spirituality of literature can be mirrored in spirituality *tout court.* Eastern ways of stillness, which have become popular as genuine aids to prayer in recent years, can also be deceptive in a gnostic direction if they fail to be entry points to a relationship of hunger and love, if they confuse self-quieting with prayer itself, and if they remain stunted as a self-trip of the interior. Once again a means becomes an end and thresholds remain uncrossed; what novelist Walker Percy calls the 'old interior itch' [12] can (to mix metaphors) become a gnostic cul-de-sac in the worlds of imagination and of meditation alike.

In both worlds one at least hopes to 'go through the concrete situation to some experience of mystery', and those words come from a letter of Flannery O'Connor, possibly the most ungnostic and indeed anti-gnostic of fiction writers of this century.[13] Her novels and stories are marvellous proof, like Olmi's film, of the possibility of an 'incarnational art' (her phrase) that differs from the mainstream of modern literature.

But, finally, one should not be too hard on gnosticism. Is it not better to be half-awake than half-asleep? It is one thing to recognise the prevalence of this mentality in modern culture. It is a further step to distinguish between varying degrees of gnostic content (in authors and works) and a gnosticism of context (in readers and audiences). But it demands a third stage of self-discernment to sort out the gnosticism of attitude entangled in many forms of spirituality today, whether literary or religious. The dividing line between icon and idol can be almost imperceptible in experience. Did it not take St Augustine nine years of gnostic involvement before he saw and seized the demon? And it was the same Ausustine who wrote a letter of extraordinary compassion about the gnostics of his day:

> Let those be angry with you who do not know with how great toil truth is to be attained, or how difficult it is to avoid mistakes. Let those be angry with you who do not know how rare

a thing it is, and how hard, to be free from the fantasies which rise up within us.

Let those be angry with you who know not how painful is the healing for the inner eye of man if it is to behold its true Sun ... Let those be angry with you who have never been led astray. (*Contra Epistolam Manichaei*)

Notes

1. T.S. Eliot, *After Strange Gods: a primer of modern heresy*, 1934, pp. 61,46,60.

2. Eliot, *On Poetry and Poets*, p. 258; Yeats cited by Richard Ellmann, *The Identity of Yeats*, 1964, p. 239.

3. Karl Rahner, *Foundations of Christian Faith*, 1978, pp. 82-83.

4. C.G. Jung, *Modern Man in Search of a Soul*, 1933, pp. 238-239.

5. Quotations from Eric Voegelin in this paragraph are taken from: *Science, Politics and Gnosticism*, 1968, p. 89; *Order and History*, Vol. ii, 1957, p. 19; *The New Sciences of Politics*, 1952, pp. 129-133; *Anamnesis*, 1978, p. 102; *From Enlightenment to Revolution*, 1975, pp. 298, 302, 273.

6. Gerald Hanratty, 'Gnosticism and Modern Thought', *Irish Theological Quarterly*, 1980, p. 129.

7. *The Autobiography of W.B. Yeats*, 1967 (Collier Books), p. 77. See Harold Bloom, 'Yeats, Gnosticism and the Sacred Void', in *Poetry and Repression*, 1976.

8. Jean Guitton, *Great Heresies and Church Councils*, 1965, pp. 53, 73, 182, 74.

9. Peter Beatson, *The Eye in the Mandala: Patrick White, a vision of man and God*, 1976, p. 167.

10. Christopher Innes, *Holy Theatre: Ritual and the Avant Garde*, 1981, p. 240.

11. Allen Tate, *Essay of Four Decades*, 1970, pp. 411, 460.

12. Percy cited by Cleanth Brooks, 'Walker Percy and Modern Gnosticism', *The Southern Review*, 1977, p. 68

13. *The Habit of Being: letters of Flannery O'Connor*, ed. Sally Fitzgerald, 1979, p. 520. In this passage she is praising William Lynch's work, especially *Christ and Apollo*, a book highly relevant to this whole argument.

PART IV: The Challenges of Latin America

There is no theology that is ideologically free.
'Let him who has no ideology cast the first stone.'
Aloysius Pieris, 1988

This fourth part brings together a number of shorter pieces, born from the author's two visits to Latin America; he spent seven months there in 1987 and another two months in 1989. As with many another person, the impact of what he witnessed there of the struggles of the poor sounded a new note for him in the chord that is faith today. The collection closes with a more spiritual essay which aims to draw some of the strands together: it reflects on the adventure of prayer within the pressures of our situation now.

Surprises of a Continent

If you look for Ecuador on a typical map of the world, you will find it well below the middle. Yet Ecuador means equator, and the midpoint of our planet runs through that country. Why then is it not in the centre of the map? Because our Mercator projections are false: they magnify the north into two-thirds of the globe, so that Europe looks larger than Latin America, even though it is smaller by nearly half.

I offer this as something of an opening parable to sum up my responses to Latin America – as a series of surprising discoveries that challenge my perspectives. It is my first visit and, as I write, I am half way through a six-month stay. So far most of my time has been spent in Venezuela but with a month in Paraguay, and brief visits to Brazil and Mexico.

My first (now humiliatingly obvious) surprise was that Latin America represents at least half the Catholic world. Perhaps I knew this as a piece of notional information but it came home to me on my first morning in Caracas, as I gazed around at the huge number of religious journals on the shelves of the Centro Gumilla (for social and theological research). They ranged from the excellent local monthly *SIC* (celebrating its 50th year) to the relatively new and more specialist *Revista Latinoamericana de Teología*. Although many books get translated, here were rich worlds of reflection whose existence is practically unknown in Europe or North America – with the possible exception of Spain. It was the first jolt to my inner Mercator map which always assumed that Europe was the intellectual centre of Catholicism.

If the shelves were full of periodicals, the streets outside were excitingly full of children and young people. This is a continent of youth, where it is normal to find forty per cent under fifteen years of age. By the year 2000 the total population may reach seven hundred million, far surpassing that of North America.

Of course the place is full of contrasts. Even in oil-rich Venezuela large majorities remain poor and some thirty per cent very poor. The centre of Caracas is all skyscrapers and fountains but the surrounding hills are lined with *ranchos*, huts that perch precariously and often collapse when the rains come. Every Sunday afternoon between five and six o'clock a strange sight can be observed: an average of seven private planes a minute fly past these *barrios* as the rich return from weekends in the islands. Out in the countryside the contrast that haunts me most is the vision of rows of oil wells, tilting constantly up and down and controlled by some distant technology, while in between them are small shacks where peasant families work the surface of the soil. Meanwhile, day and night, the depths of their own land yields up its wealth to the government and to the fluctuations of the world market.

Shrines and Statues

Putting the massive Catholicism of this continent over against its all too visible social divisions, one asks the obvious question: what kind of Church is to be found now in Latin America? I think it is fair to say that there are three faces to the Church here – the traditional parish, the world of popular religiousnes, and the liberation minority.

About the first there is no need to say much. This largely clerical model can be found everywhere in the world, served by priests whose pastoral focus is sacraments and preaching. It ranges here as elsewhere from being imaginative, friendly and nourishing to being authoritarian, ritualistic and empty. One of the surprises of Latin America was that this model was still so frequent and that the liberation one, about which I will say more in a further article, remains in practice a most influential but minority phenomenon.

The Church of *religiosidad popular* was so new to me that I want to pause on it and devote the remainder of this essay to its significance. On my first day in Caracas I was brought to see some city centre churches and was amazed to find a constant flow of people to shrines and suffering statues of hyper-realism. Indeed, these seemed much more 'popular' than the Blessed Sacrament chapel. Moreover, the people were of all ages and classes. I saw young men kneeling at mid-morning before St Rita, or hand-holding teenage couples with lips moving before the Sacred Heart. Outside, many of those who might not actually enter would pause a moment to salute a statue in the doorway. And this was in a continent where – as one French priest in Brazil told me with Gallic irony – a smaller proportion of the population go to Sunday Mass than in France

Such devotionalism remained for me a strange and alien sight until the day when I stopped being a mere observer. It happened that I had to wait for an office to open and decided to spend the hour next door in the vast Basilica of St Teresa, probably the most popular church in Caracas. Instead of trying to pray with eyes closed, I chose to enter into the comings and goings around me in a spirit of reverence. I saw a man who reminded me, for some reason, of a night-club bouncer, standing with eyes fixed on the Virgin in unselfconscious intimacy. I noticed a thin young man of indigenous Indian face moving slowly from statue to statue, touching each for some time. In the middle of all this, Mass was going on. A worn woman in poorish clothing went straight from receiving communion in order to push a flower into the lap of a Virgin and Child, and stood there as if in deep conversation. For a moment my judgmental self took over: 'what ignorance of the Eucharist to mix it with such pietism'. But that reaction was silenced by the sheer transparency of the woman's faith; watching her with reverence, I found myself invited into something of the wavelength of the Beatitudes.

The extrovert temperament is not universal in Latin America. There are many forms of popular religiousness, ranging from the custom of asking a blessing from one's parents each day to the nine days of family prayer leading up to the anniversary of a death. Much of it is independent of the official Church and survives by strong family inheritance.

During Holy Week I lived in a *barrio* of Asunción (Paraguay) where more formal and communal expressions of religiousness reigned – perhaps because of the peasant background and indigenous heritage of many of the people. Each night groups of twelve men, representing the apostles, went round with candles, singing ancient Passion hymns, and pausing at the simple altars placed in front of every hut. On Good Friday no fires were lit for cooking and on Holy Saturday no meat was eaten either and the children were not to run around on this day of mourning with the Virgin. Side by side with Asunción, the Caracas devotions seemed more private and poorer in community. My Holy Week world reminded me of that great film, Olmi's *Tree of the Wooden Clogs*, where a culture of peasant faith exposes the impoverishment of our modernities.

About such a religiousness many questions remain. Where does faith end and superstition begin? How can these customs become fruitful in a liberation sense? With the impact of urbanisation, will not these symbols become eroded and feeble? What hope of survival has such piety in a continent being invaded by both the junk culture and the equally junk evangelism of North America?

Even if it is ambiguous or endangered, this popular religiousness remains a powerful strand in the Catholicism of Latin America. My own initial shock gave way to a hunch that there is a wise theology behind it all – rooted in an intuition of a God of care and closeness, an unlonely God who has a community of many friends.

Living Liberation

Do any hymns sung in the English-speaking world contain the word 'organise'? I doubt it. But that word is often sung with fervour at Masses in Latin America – perhaps not in the more traditional parishes, but certainly in the many smaller groups that gather round the word of God. There people sing and pray for the courage to organise in their struggles for justice. If 'organise' seems too political for our more tame hymnbooks, across the South Atlantic it is often accompanied by a more religious word, but one that can now cause unease in English – 'sin'. In Latin America, however, sin is all too visible – in the impoverishment of the majority, in the violence of the state, and even in the sluggish conversion of the Church itself to the liberation options it bravely voiced in Medellin and Puebla.

Any visitor to Latin America who expects to find a Church dramatically united in the liberation mould is bound to be disappointed. The continent reveals many divisions within the Church. The public tensions in Nicaragua between most of the bishops and most of the religious are echoed, if less acutely, elsewhere. Nevertheless, in my few months in Latin America I have found the leaven of liberation everywhere at work behind the scenes, even if it remains as yet a minority influence.

Latin America is the natural home of liberation theology, born from scandals and from positive sources that are both at their strongest here – from the 'sin' of social systems that oppress, and from the deep faith of a people that can 'organise' to change their world. Volumes are written about the significance of liberation theology. It is defined in many ways. One of the shortest and best that I know comes from Marie Augusta Neal: 'the living Church finding God with the organising poor seeking social justice'. Certainly my guess is that it is evangelically simple in its roots; later it becomes a way of re-reading revelation and reality. In this article I want to communicate not so much the theory as the practice, by describing what I have seen and heard in my short time here so far.

My first glimpse of the leaven of liberation came from attending Sunday morning Mass in a poor *barrio*, and from discovering various customs there that would be most unlikely in the average large parish anywhere in the world. First, there is active participation by the community, and in particular a wide-ranging sharing in the homily or scripture reflection. All sorts of issues were raised as part of an invitation to seek out the signs of death and of new life in the everyday world: the inequalities of the medical services, the shortage of water, the doubling of the price of transport, how teachers were being pushed into strike action unwillingly, a local incident of aggression by police, a child who had begun to write at last, the success of the youth magazine in the area, a bake-your-own-bread scheme starting, the community spirit in the *barrio* during Holy Week.

Life not Libraries

What was more surprising still was the dialogue between these realities and the word of God. I noticed a reversal of the familiar advice to look at life in the light of the Scriptures; here was a reading of Scripture in the light of reality. This reverse flow seemed to work both in the context of the Eucharist and in the more open agenda of community gatherings. One Sunday afternoon group met in a schoolroom, where I remember the transparently generous presence of Fernanda, a large woman in her fifties, who was the acknowledged leader of the whole *barrio*: she sat there not saying much but her eyes aflame with interest over every detail of the people and of the Gospel we were exploring. Another group met at night on the steps of an extremely poor *rancho*. A young catechist called Orlando arrived, perspiring from the heat and straight from his evening classes, to share his excitement about one sentence in the raising of Lazarus: if you believe, you will see God's glory. And he went on to describe the glory of God in the hopes of the struggling poor.

As it happened, my early weeks in Latin America coincided with an extraordinary sequence of scripture texts for the Sundays and other feasts – extraordinary in that they lent themselves to being heard from the perspective of the poor. The Beatitudes, in the present tense, rang true of the people there. The Simeon scene (like many of Luke's infancy stories) now spoke of a man waiting for liberation, surprised by recognising God in a poor child, and able to acknowledge also the road of conflict ahead. Hearing about salt losing its taste, I could not but think of the lifelessness of the same liturgy in so many more privileged settings, and of the alive community within which I was hearing the Gospel now. Likewise the text about leaving one's offering and first being reconciled came across as one of the many emphatic biblical statements on the priority of the practice of religion over religious practices.

Here were the required readings fresh with life from the angle of the poor, and sounding like a planned course in liberation spirituality. Some of the fundamentals were there in simple form. Liberation theology starts from realities lived by the poor, and on the basis of this shared experience, it re-reads the Gospel as a call to action. Its many other strands stem from this basic stance: recognising that evil systems are not the will of God; facing the facts of conflict and sin; rebelling against all forms of passivity in society and frozen rituals in religion; staying close to the history of Jesus and discerning the continuing history of God acting to set his people free. Much could be added but what I discovered in those many groups of believers was a triple encounter of struggle, sharing and Scripture – and it was quiet dynamite to behold in action in the community of the poor.

Again and again I found myself recalling the prophetic words of King Lear, when that pampered old man is confronted for the first time with the poverty of his people. In the storm he is himself without a roof for the night and comes to a personal revelation:

I have ta'en
Too little care of this. Take physic, pomp;
Expose thyself to feel what wretches feel,
That thou mayst shake the superflux to them,
And show the heavens more just.

There is extraordinary richness of insight here and a whole process of conversion: the shock of poverty as experienced; the emphasis on feeling solidarity; the freedom to let go of what previously seemed essential, and even the suggestion that one is demonstrating a different face of God, through a different distribution of the world's goods.

So does this leaven of liberation have any impact on those in Latin America who are not poor? I limit myself to one example, the story of a well-off lady called Carmel, an opera singer whose family had grown up and who decided to take a course in theology. It so changed her, in Zacchaeus fashion, that now all her energies go into three experimental schools that she has founded in the least reachable part of a high *barrio* in Caracas. She organises fund-raising and manages to challenge the conscience of some of her richer friends and raise their awareness, getting them to visit the schools and the extremely poor families around. The first day she brought me there, we were greeted in each classroom with huge delight by the children. I will not easily forget the loud chorus of answers to Carmel's questions: Why did Jesus come? To begin the Kingdom! And what does the Kingdom mean? Justice! And what is justice? Sharing with one another! In that chorus of happy children – both in the content and in the context – one has a pretty good short summary of liberation theory and practice.

So I think – and hope – that my experience of the leaven of liberation is expanding my own horizons of faith. Looking back at how I tried to grapple with issues of loss of faith, I now wonder if I did not miss an obvious source of unbelief in our Western world: is it not a natural by-product of an egoist system, whose propaganda dominates our culture? If so, the real answers to atheism will come not so much in print as in practice. You do not arrive at faith by thinking it out but by living it out, or as St John's gospel puts it, 'whoever does the truth comes into the light' (Jn 3:21).

That is one of the key lessons of liberation in Latin America – that its origin is not in libraries but in life. Jon Sobrino described one of the Ratzinger statements on liberation as *un documento sin patria,* as lacking roots of solidarity and struggle. There are many typewriter theologians of liberation. The real prophets are those who come in from the field and sit down to write with sweat on their brows or tears in their eyes. And sometimes they are called to pay a more total price.

Assassination and St Anthony

Venezuela: a Sunday in the second half of August, 1989.

I was in Barquisimeto, which is about 200 miles west of Caracas, and was due to say Mass in the local *barrio* in an open shed where about 200 people would gather. I had done so once before and the occasion had gone well, helped by the charm of my faltering Spanish and with a student priest to lead people in their customary shared reflections. But this time I was uneasy about the undertaking. For one thing the Gospel of the day was a difficult one, about Jesus casting fire on the earth, not bringing peace but division. So when a local priest, called Alejo, happened to be available, I was happy to let him take my place.

'Menos mal,' as I said to friends afterwards: just as well. I do not know how I could have handled the situation that presented itself. Watching my substitute in action was a lesson both in liturgy and in how Latin America is different. A minor surprise was that without notice there was a girl, aged about 12, for First Communion. She was introduced and applauded. Then as Mass was beginning, the big gate of the shed opened to allow in a procession bearing a flower-bedecked table with a statue of St Anthony. It must be a promise, the old lady beside me explained, adding that there would be singing and dancing for the saint afterwards.

Up to the front went the procession, accompanied by some 20 young men with white hats and guitars, followed by girls in long dresses, and children painted in Indian fashion. Alejo greeted them all and explained that this was an act of thanksgiving for a successful operation of a little girl, who now shared the front bench with the first communicant.

Then came an amazing change of tone. Alejo asked people to spend some time in quiet, getting ready to hear a challenging Gospel. He then invited them to voice their reactions to the news of the day before, the assassination in neighbouring Colombia of a leading presidential candidate. The carnival atmosphere gave way to gravity. For up to half an hour people spoke in threes and fours and then in the full congregation about the evils surrounding them in Latin America. Colombia has an average of 20 killings a day, related either to social struggles or to the drug barons. This was the face of sin, of injustice, the contrary of the Kingdom, the rule of big money from the empire in the North, the trampling on the hopes of the poor, yet another martyrdom.

Right, said Alejo, now let us hear the Gospel being read in Colombia and in the whole world today. The effect was a stunned silence. It was so relevant and so tough. It needed no commentary.

Christ's kind of peace was born of fire, of baptism, of the cost of taking sides. The words of Luke (12:49-53) were themselves on fire in that chapel shed. With that extended preparation, the prayers and central offering of the Eucharist now flowed as something genuine and quietly dramatic.

At its close St Anthony took over in yet another shift of mood. First there was an ancient hymn of thanksgiving as people gathered round the saint. There followed processional music as the statue was taken down the road to the house of the girl whose recovery was being celebrated. The Mass might be over but the thanksgiving was only beginning. In the street beside the house was a roped-off area for formal dancing in front of the statue. All the dances began with the couples blessing themselves and bowing before the saint who was so much part of the proceedings that, at one stage when the dancers were sharing a bottle of rum, he too had some thrown over him. No doubt noticing my raised Celtic eyebrow, my neighbour explained that, as our friends, the saints are involved in every aspect of life, even rum. And indeed these dances, all of pre-colonial origin, dramatised a range of situations between men and women – from playfulness to conflict, from love to death.

During the Mass the murder in Colombia had been the springboard for hearing the Gospel afresh. Now in the street a similar intermingling of faith and life was taking place. Perhaps I should add a comic confession. Alejo could not come to the thanksgiving dance at the house. So at the insistence of the grandmother a chair was produced for me, and there I sat in solitary priestly dignity beside St Anthony – except that I was given no rum.

As I sat there I pondered again – as I had done on my first visit – the paleness of our Western worship. Here among poor people was a more living liturgy than is normal in our comfortable churches. It had faced the pain of public evil. It had gathered the joys of the people. It had built a prayerful and alert bridge between the realities of life and the words of Scripture. Above all, it had been a community event. This is one face of the Church in Latin America, a blend of the populist, the traditional and the liberationist. Sadly, it is a combination under some pressure and suspicion.

Church of Clashing Symbols

A baptism ceremony was under way on Saturday afternoon in the eighteenth-century church of a small town called Quibor. The middle-aged priest was speaking quietly into the microphone but the congregation looked distant and tense. His message was stark: if a man and woman are not properly married in church, each of them is living with the devil. And this in Venezuela where well over half the babies for baptism come from such unions.

Next morning a newspaper article by the local bishop struck a different note. He wrote about the burden of external debt crippling the country and criticised the remedies of the International Monetary Fund as a 'neo-liberal offensive with its baggage of individualism' showing 'no sensitivity for the social cost of its packages'. This was the Venezuela where over a thousand were killed in the first few days of March after the poor of the *barrios* rioted in direct response to price rises imposed at the bidding of the IMF. In four days the army of this respected and oil-rich democracy used four million bullets mainly against the sections of its people who live in 'critical' poverty.

A similar gap between different perceptions of faith showed itself a few months ago when CELAM (the body of bishops for the continent) clashed with CLAR (the parallel body representing the many religious in Latin America) over the latter's *Palabra-Vida* (Word-Life). This was intended as a contribution to the celebration in 1992 of the fifth centenary of the evangelisation of Latin America. Its stated aim was 'to nourish life with the Word of God, read from the perspective of the poor'. But CELAM accused the document of manipulating Scripture in favour of a social and political interpretation of Latin America as divided into oppressors and oppressed. The Vatican Congregation for Religious also issued a note against the 'unilateral' biblical method used. Particular objection was taken to one sentence which was thought reductive of salvation history in Christ: 'The main certainty that the Bible communicates in this: God listens to the cry of his oppressed people.'

This clash seems symptomatic of divisions not so much in theology as in the shaping experiences that give rise to theologising. The starting-points for reflection are different. Academic fine combs (this is my own public confession of twenty years) can easily pick out careless sentences – at least in one sense of 'care'. In another sense of the word, Bishop Tomas Balduino of Brazil has voiced his fear of a second Middle Ages if the Vatican's misunderstanding of basic communities continues. Compared with the first-hand experiences that foster a commitment to liberation, the distance of a desk, Roman or otherwise, lends itself to merely verbal anxieties. The person behind a desk can lack the lived contacts with the poor that would give another tone to 'care'. One sees life from where one is; each life-style has its own prejudices and priorities. Diverging pastoral vocabularies are rooted in quite different spiritual geographies.

In this connection I often heard talk of the appointment of 'conservative' bishops as a means of containing the liberation tendency, which continues to get its strength from men and women religious involved with basic ecclesial communities. But I relish the true story of a newly appointed bishop who came, in somewhat inquisitorial mood, to visit one of those communities. He began by asking them to define the three terms (base, ecclesial, community). They could not even begin. It was not their language. But when he asked them to explain in their own way what they were doing, he ended up impressed and at peace. He found himself listening to simple rather than learned people (the contrast of Mt. 11:25), hearing how they came together in a community of faith and how they discovered the Bible as giving them power in their struggles.

The liberation theologian who recounted this incident to me added: 'In our groups I have never heard the word "liberation" or the word "theology".' He said that if it would lessen the level of worry in high Church circles, he would gladly abandon the now loaded term 'liberation'. For him it referred primarily to a community spirituality, or way of experiencing one's faith together, and only in the second place to a theology, or way of interpreting that experience. Those who are not directly in contact with the basic communities will inevitably get the wrong end of the stick and may suspect them of being too ideological. When written down, 'liberation' can seem too shrill, or just careless. But in the Catholic communities of 'underlined bibles', as they have been called, what is central is a regular solidarity in faith, a spirituality of social hope. In this they contrast with those other bible groups which have proliferated in Latin America in recent years: these, evangelical, fundamentalist and backed by North American finance, interpret the text in a individualistic and anti-social way.

The Church has a crucial role to play in the shaping of history for this most Catholic of continents. Therefore the clash of faith languages is more than academic. It can be literally a matter of life and death. So let me end with another quotation from a radical bishop. 'You cannot separate evangelisation from the work of justice, proclaiming the Kingdom from promoting it. With your witness the forgotten may feel solidarity, the voiceless may be heard, and those unjustly treated may find defence and help.' That bishop, speaking to priests, religious and seminarians in Paraguay in 1988, was Pope John Paul.

Looking North At a World of Self

There is no such thing as society –
there are individual men and women and there are families.
Margaret Thatcher

At home in Ireland I often reviewed Woody Allen movies, usually with admiration. Now I find myself wanting to comment on his work again, but from a strangely different perspective, as I spend six months of a sabbatical in Latin America.

To see *Hannah and Her Sisters* down here was a bit confusing. Yes, it was a pleasure to see Woody Allen at his best – playful, ironic, profound. But ... I want to voice my new doubts about everything he stands for, a culture that I have been at home in most of my adult life.

I add that last qualification because I grew up in a village in the west of Ireland during the simple years of the 1940's and 1950's. Out of that world I emerged in the 1960's to become a fully paid-up member of the international educated club, enthusing about Bellow and Beckett and Bergman in one breath. My village became part of forgotten past, its culture disowned with a certain indecent haste. But being in Latin America has meant re-entering that first culture of mine, and watching Woody Allen here has awakened many questions about the over-weening self of my second culture.

Most people in Latin America cannot afford subjectivity: they have neither the inner nor the outer space for it. Their life struggles are more basic, and yet their life supports are more real.

Woody, by comparison, is worried about many things (including his own solitary God), but his whole world is one of self, indeed of imprisoned subjectivity. There may be excursions into relationships, but they too seem closed and fragile twosomes within a society of hassle. Viewed from down here, everybody in *Hannah and Her Sisters* seems hyper-conscious of his or her own little self. Everybody has the tools – of leisure and lucre – to dabble with experiments of a subjective kind, whether it be the adventure of an affair, the game of catering, a flirtation with religious conversion, autobiography or swapping sisters as wives. All these are attempts to escape from a variety of private prisons: alcoholism, cocaine addiction, cynicism, hypocondria, infertility, infidelities and the angst of mortality.

When I came out of the movie into the streets, I ran into my questions, questions born of my last four months in Latin America. They stemmed, for instance, from my experience of living for a while in a *barrio* shack with other Jesuits. It was never private, with a constant stream of neighbours dropping in, and always children who came to play, to chat, to hope for food or just to sit and watch. (The few children in *Hannah* seemed spoiled and silent by comparison.) Another memory, taken almost at random as I write, is of bringing Communion to an old man close to death in a *rancho* or hut. Sitting up in bed, he had much to say about his life and God, as his relations of all ages crowded in the doorway with marvellous affection in their eyes. In the midst of poverty, not dire but acute nonetheless, this was community, family, faith and death without fear. (The lavish Thanksgiving gatherings in *Hannah* seemed brittle and full of forced jollity.)

I wonder whether the blind spots in *Hannah* might not be those of a whole way of life in which reality shrinks to the psychological or the subjective. Does this happen by accident? Before coming to Latin America, I might have said of Woody Allen that he has problems about God because his consciousness is too crowded and because his images of God seem too philosophical. It is more obvious from down here why God gets eclipsed in a culture that promotes the self but blocks the spirit.

What does this mean? It is close to a contrast of two worlds that Feodor Dostoevsky made in 1863. After a visit to London, he returned to Russia and set down his *Winter Notes on Summer Impressions*; he described the city as an 'anthill', but what had disturbed him most was the Crystal Palace, built to house the Great Exhibition, which summed up for him all the ugly pride of a commercial empire. As he put it, a rich tradition of protest would be needed if one were to resist this 'worship of fact'. Going further, he discerned the root of this whole world as the 'principle of individual isolation' and hence of 'self-seeking'. In brief, he had seen a system that in his view was hostile to the Gospel. He had discerned something dehumanising and idolatrous in the assumptions of Western society.

Perhaps Dostoevsky's critique of our culture remains accurate even today; therefore the incredibility of God (an Allen obsession) comes as no surprise. For all its disorders and deprivations, Latin America seems better able to foster some basics of faith. We Northerners have often been told that we are 'lonely crowds' or 'people of the lie' – in the sense of being starved for community and unable to own the truth of our sin. From down here, both accusations seem valid, but a third can be suggested. Certainly, Latin America preserves a stronger sense of togetherness, which is especially exciting in the many 'basic communities' of the Church here. And this Catholic continent is evolving a wider sense of sin – as something all too tangible in unnecessary poverty, political corruption, institutional violence and even murder of the innocent. A third fundamental of faith, absent from the Woody Allen world, is the quality that the gospels describe as 'childhood' or 'poverty of spirit'. Down here, there is much poverty and there are many children, and there is something essential to be learned from the presence of both.

I am sometimes asked if I am learning anything from the poor, and I find myself saying – 'a tone for faith'. The setting of poverty seems to guard a natural sense of Christ, a different reading of the gospels, a far-from-simplistic trust in a God of love and often a movingly generous sharing of what one has with others. In saying this, there is the danger of romanticising an evil: there is a negative poverty that is stark injustice, but there is a positive poverty that is freedom for faith. Paradoxically, the two often seem to go together. Looking back at *Hannah and Her Sisters*, I saw little real community, a hiding from sin and destructiveness and nothing of either kind of poverty; no wonder that the 'child' of the gospels remained untapped, suppressed within an inflated self.

By way of postcript: a similar retreat into subjectivity occurs at the very end of *Platoon* when, after a powerful exposure of the systems of war, a moralising voice tells us that the real war is within the self. From down here one does not deny that personalist truth – but other truths demand to be heard.

Prayer: Ringing the Changes

Prayer is less petition or communication
than this daily structuring of our minds to permit God's entrance.
Emil Antonucci

The word *change* in the title can point in at least two different directions. If I am committed to some regular life of prayer, then the changing situation of each day will need a constant creativity, for the obvious reason that I can only pray as I am today and not from how I might like to be. These changes in the short-term are not our main focus here; this essay will deal with changes in the long-term – how the passing of the years naturally calls forth some evolution in one's way of praying. If I lack the courage to follow these invitations, short-term or long-term, prayer easily becomes 'stuck', and it is hard not to abandon the effort sooner or later. So these pages are really about imagination and courage in the adventure of prayer. As Thomas Merton once said, 'Progress in prayer is a continual burning of bridges behind us.'

Probably everybody would agree that personal prayer is meant to become more simple with the years. This seems to be both obvious in theory and hard to accept in practice. We seem to be conservatives in prayer, often harking back to what used to 'work' and feeling disappointed when it seems so seldom to 'work' now. So what I want to offer here is a list of 'transitions' that seem typical in this process of prayer becoming more simple. Not all of the transitions need apply to any one individual and certainly they are unlikely to happen all at once. But some of them seem to be part of the experience of many people: to recognise them as normal can help a person to trust his or her experience and to see these invitations as the promptings of the Spirit.

These few paragraphs are not intended as a treatise in spiritual theology, nor as a summary of the great experts in prayer. What is intended here is more personal – gathered from my own unsteady efforts to pray and enriched by having had occasion to listen to the experience of others as well.

I relish the story of a colleague of mine who was on a visit to a Carthusian community for some weeks. Towards the end of his stay, his attention was caught by one monk who seemed to radiate a certain inner strength and was even more of a hermit than the others. My friend sought an audience with this holy man and, after telling him of the busy life that he was about to return to, asked advice on how to pray better. The hermit looked at him and said, 'Pray in, not up'.

And bade him farewell. My friend, after his elaborate outline of his dilemma, was given but four words of wisdom! But that tantalising reply provides me with the first of the series of 'transitions' that I want to suggest as in-built within the usual life-cycle of prayer.

From God outside me to God inside me

No doubt God is everywhere, but when I begin to pray, my limited imagination tends to picture the One to whom I come as located somewhere or other. What the Carthusian was suggesting to his client was that he focus primarily on the presence of the Spirit within him. Clearly this advice is rooted in the scriptures in many places – in the promise of Jesus at the Last Supper that his Spirit would be 'with' and 'within' his disciples, or the passage in St Paul where he envisages the Spirit struggling within us when we do not know how to pray (Jn 14:17; Rom 8:26). In short, a new awareness of the in-dwelling of God in our hearts is one of many simplifications that seem to happen with the years.

From 'God' to Trinity

There is a parallel invitation to move from God as one to God as three. Putting this personally, I can clearly remember studying the Trinity in theology and indeed doing some ambitious essay on the doctrine as it evolved through the early centuries. But it was years later before it became spiritually alive for me and in fact has become one of the central enthusiasms of my faith. Probably it was a simple realisation that the solemn prayers of the Mass are so rootedly Trinitarian that began slowly to influence my perception of personal prayer. The crucial image here is the Gospel picture of Jesus led by the Spirit and praying to the Father on the mountain. Gradually I came to realise that Christian prayer is always an echo of that encounter: I am invited by the Spirit to be with Jesus before the Father. And being with Jesus involves being in solidarity with his people – which links this transition with the two last ones to be outlined below.

From Speaking to Listening

Here is an obvious and often mentioned growth-point in prayer. It is voiced by Jesus himself in the advice not to use many words but it seems to be one of the crucial thresholds for people in the expansion of their prayer lives. It needs a certain courage to let go of the security of conversational prayer and of familiar images in order to enter less familiar zones of silence. But silence is the language of God and this transition is a vital step towards a more contemplative level of prayer. It means an emergence from self-strength to a trust that God is 'there' in all his strange shyness. One's own resources have proved painfully incapable of bearing fruit any more (even if they once did). Then it is time to let go of 'the perpetual monologue of the ego'

(Laurence Freeman) and to let down the nets into deeper water.

In my experience this transition comes slowly – so that prayer can be a mixture of old and new wavelengths. But the wisdom of the contemplative tradition seems unanimous on this point, that a time comes, sooner or later, when more 'chatty' forms of active prayer become boring, and this is usually a sign that it is right to let go of one's self-controlled agenda and to risk a quieter listening. Unfortunately many people experience only the sense of strandedness and do not know how to read it as a positive signal to move on. It is sad if they throw in the sponge and abandon the whole enterprise as not-for-them.

From Forgetting to Remembering the Body

As a practical help towards that deeper listening, the last decade or two of spiritual writing has seen an explosion of interest in learning from the East, and more particularly a popularising of various skills of stillness that start from the physical.

Many anchors can be suggested to root the scattered self and lead towards the threshold of prayer, for instance the sound of a mantra, the rhythm of one's breathing, the flame of a candle. What they have in common is an acknowledgement of the bodily basis of being ready to give 'loving attentiveness' to God (to use the famous phrase of John of the Cross). Certainly these techniques could degenerate into narcissistic 'trips' of consciousness, becoming ends instead of means, with the result that real prayer – as relationship and dialogue – simply fails to happen.

But dangers aside, this renewed awareness of the body brings many advantages. It can be a practical 're-collection' for prayer and indeed a form of reverence for the humanity of each person as body-spirit. In today's culture with its avalanche of silly images, some such techniques seem crucial as a kind of self-ecology, because the environment of our spiritual awareness needs just as much protection from pollution as our rivers and seas. Again, where an older spirituality seemed to ignore the body, these newer versions of wisdom can help people to ground their praying in a steadier silence and to escape what the Zen masters call the 'cave of conceptualisation'. Thus prayer may have a better chance of going beyond self-homilies (and often negative self-homilies at that). 'Lose your mind and come to your senses' was one of the characteristic de Mello ways of capturing this gateway to listening to God.

From Asking to Offering

Thomas Aquinas remarked that prayer is the language of desire, and there is no doubt that prayer of petition is a central strand in the Christian tradition. And yet it is not the whole story. Asking to know the love of God leads on to offering oneself to the struggle of loving. Something of this transition can be found even in the great scene of the Annunciation. Mary is at first the receiver of a gift, indeed a disturbing gift as Luke stresses. But the scene moves through questions and struggle to surrender. Mary ends by offering herself to the hopes of God. And this note too is a vital one in the chord that is prayer. It is an essential part of the journey of prayer to move towards a fuller degree of availability for God and for the tasks of life – as in the spirit of the concluding offering of the *Spiritual Exercises* of Ignatius Loyola, 'Take and receive ... all that I am'.

From 'My' to 'Our'

Another healthy transition would be from a me-alone-with-God model of prayer to a humbler sense of not being separate from the human drama as I enter a space of quiet. Perhaps a good deal of what we have called 'personal' prayer has been in fact so 'private' as to be unfaithful to the Lord's own prayer, which of course begins with the word 'our'. In this respect, an almost infallible way to liberate our praying from a cul-de-sac of introspection is to have exposure to the suffering of the poor. Even to say this is risky because it could colonise the poor into fodder for 'my' pious feelings. But a genuine conversion from 'my' to 'our' is a grace, born from some steady contact with the struggles of people.

If I come to prayer having encountered during this day the pain of oppression, the call of that experience can gather me before God better than any Eastern 'onepointedness'. To approach prayer from having spent time with an AIDS victim, or visited a prison, or met with family agony, or witnessed the ravages of unemployment, or touched the suffering of children in a *barrio* anywhere in the world ... to see any of the daily faces of woundedness must give birth to a more plural prayer and one that disturbs my complacencies.

The experience of situations like these forces the Christian to emerge from self-concern into solidarity of some kind, and the cry of such realities cannot but give a different tone to his or her prayer. The praying will come more from below than from above. Two graces can come through this more inserted prayer: first, I need a grace of sorrow over the systems of sin that weigh down on most of humanity; next I can seek a grace of sharing the always creative and at times angry compassion of the heart of Christ. A prayer of this kind comes to the Lord carrying burdens, not mine only but ours, and seeks to 'expand the size of one's tent' (Is 54:2).

From cut-off to committed

Linked with this alertness to injustice, sometimes an objection to the whole business of personal prayer stems from feeling it to be divorced from reality. If it is experienced as an escapist withdrawal, many an actively generous person will become disillusioned. It is one thing to admit that prayer need not produce tangible results; it is quite another thing to sense over time that one's praying has no worthwhile impact on one's life. Once this deeper uselessness is suspected, it can rob prayer of any energy or enthusiasm. And yet it is just this crisis that can spark off a purification and another necessary transition. What God do I pray to really? That is a fruitful if disturbing question, because behind cramped prayer often lurk cramped images of God. Behind the sense that my inner life remains 'cut-off' from reality can lie an image of God as distant and passive, a God who seems more interested in my pious awareness of his presence than One who wants to change hearts and transform the world. I can vividly remember the shock I felt listening to a sermon in Latin America which insisted that Jesus was not much concerned with God; instead the axis of his life was the Kingdom of God. In other words he was forever pointing people towards the hopes of God to be more real within human history (as well as beyond it). To encounter this Christ, and especially to encounter the call of the Kingdom through situations of oppression, makes one naturally dissatisfied with any narrowly 'spiritual' version of prayer.

The awareness of God, central in prayer, can remain like an island, but in fact cries out to become a bridge to action. To take the metaphor further, the bridge is one for two-way traffic: not only is there the flow of compassion born from contemplation but there is the other flow of a hunger born from involvement with the sufferings and struggles of people. Prayer flourishes not as escape but as energy, not as witdrawal but as an inclusiveness that can embrace all of human reality. The love lesson with God that is prayer remains dishonest unless it takes flesh in life as lived, just as life as lived – both as generosity and as failure – can be the springboard for a more genuine and integrated prayer.

A Set of Invitations

To talk glibly of these 'transitions' entails a danger of idealising. The nitty-gritty of trying to pray never obeys such over-simple outlines. Nevertheless these headings seem to point to some of the key invitations to expansion in prayer life that goes on into the middle years (which is anything from thirty onwards according to my students). In my experience these transitions can come and go many times and can happen with no predictable pattern. It seems akin to some of the research on faith development associated with James Fowler. He would hold that the language of faith – how it is felt and lived – undergoes a number of crucial shifts as life proceeds. Of relevance to our topic here is the move from what he calls Stage IV to Stage V in faith development, one which involves leaving behind clarities and entering what seems at first a bewildering experience of confusion and darkness.

This is a spiritual version of the mid-life crisis (a theme explored by Gerald O'Collins in *The Second Journey*). It is marked not only by entering into a more painful cloud of unknowing but by an opportunity for a new wisdom that links contemplation and compassion. The invitation is to let go of some of the securities of the past and to feel at home with the strangeness of God's silence. It is a moment when a person can arrive at a more serene acceptance of human frailty, one's own and that of other people. And yet it is a time that can open new doors into a socially committed faith and a socially nourished prayer.

'Love you as you love me?' wrote Therese of Lisieux. 'The only way to do that is to come to you for a loan of your own love'. The childlike transparency of that phrase is a reminder of the simple heart of all Christian prayer, whatever form it takes or whatever the phase of life. I find the same insight, expressed differently, in the Spanish writer Gomez Caffarena, who says that the key to all prayer is to love with God (*amar con Dios*). The drama that is prayer always starts, whether the pray-er is conscious of this or not, from the gift of God's love for us. In one sense it is misleading to think of prayer as us reaching out to God. God does the first reaching always. That love is from above first in order to be from below afterwards. It is the one love that flows down and out, so to speak.

I think of that flow of God's love as an upside-down capital T, where one vertical line comes down and two lines go out. The point where the lines meet is where prayer happens, where I receive love in order to give love. So to pray is to relax into the reality of being loved by God and to rise then into the slow reality of loving. It is through prayer that the heart learns how to love a little like God.

But this article has become dangerously eloquent. Words about prayer are easy. The daily adventure of trying to pray is not so simple. Johann Baptist Metz has written a powerful passage in *The Emergent Church* about our reducing love to an idol, to 'a mere belief in love', to a cosy idea. It is possible to write – or read – an article like this out of a mere belief in prayer. Let us pray to keep searching out honest ways to pray – for 'God unworshipped withers to the Futile One' (Patrick Kavanagh).

Epilogue

Prison and Library
Broadcast as a Radio Reflection in May 1989;
now dedicated to the memory of T.G. who died four months later.

A few days ago I found myself in prison – visiting I mean. T had only recently been sent to jail (in a rushed trial when, after waiting two hours, I was not let speak in his defence). He was still in a state of shock – not eating much, hardly sleeping at all. We talked for the half an hour we were allowed and I hope it helped. I left that prison with the images of the place powerfully in my mind – the silent line of young faces, the trays of dinner carried off to solitary cells, the drawn look of my friend. Those pictures haunted me as I walked away into the streets.

An hour later I found myself in a very different place, looking up references in a university library. There surrounded by other young faces, many of them looking a bit worn with exams approaching, I sat absorbed in front of an electronic catalogue – no old-fashioned cards here – and chased up titles. Until the spell broke, so to speak, and the pictures of prison returned. It was another world, only a mile away.

Was there any bridge, I found myself wondering, between the two places? Was life all fragments with nothing to hold it together? T will probably never in his life set foot inside a university library. Could there be any real connection between the two scenes? All I knew is that the unity would have to be bigger than me, somehow beyond me.

A strange coincidence led to a hint of an answer. On the bus home, I opened the New Testament and hit on a sentence in Colossians: 'in him all things hold together.' I say I hit on the sentence. In fact it hit me. I knew on the bus that Christ unites prison and library – if only I open and allow. The Jesus of the gospels would more likely visit a prison than a library. But the Christ of now was asking me, somehow, to do both, to search those books in a way that would be faithful to my friend in prison. To do everything in tune with His compassion for the wounded of the world. Which alone holds the bits together.